BLUNT F

Alice,

Sisters in Sobriety

One Day at a time.

Gail Huntley

2012

One Day at a time.

ii

BLUNT FORCE WINDS

BY

GAIL HUNTLEY

**Cover Photo: Mt. Sabattis, Long Lake, New York,
by James Swedberg**

**www.GailHuntley.com
www.gailonwritingabook.blogspot.com**

www.bookstandpublishing.com

Published by
Bookstand Publishing
Morgan Hill, CA 95037
3588_5

DISCLAIMER

All of the events recounted in this book are true. However, in certain
sensitive instances, the names of individuals and locations have been
changed in order to protect the identities of those individuals.

ISBN 978-1-61863-176-3

Printed in the United States of America

ACKNOWLEDGEMENTS

First, I would like to thank my sister, Venita, for her encouragement, care, and love throughout my life, and for always being there to pick up the pieces. I would like to thank my family for their wisdom and help during this endeavor. My courageous brother, Mike for saying, "Just write your heart out," and for coming home from Vietnam a hero and alive. Larry, you have always been my hero. Sheryl, thank you for living with me off and on, sharing sister secrets, and being the beautiful person you are. Ricky and Monti, thank you for loving me through the good times and bad and giving me three awesome grandchildren.

I could not have written this book without the help of the friends in the program that saved my life, so I give honor to the fellowship, especially my sponsors and close women friends.

I want to thank my childhood friends Bobbie, Gloria S, Gloria G, and Joany for letting me tell the truth and helping me clarify many details.

Thank you, Jeff Rutherford, for your excellent editing expertise, and encouragement. Jim Swedberg, thank you for your patience and beautiful photography.

Thank you, Andrew, at Bookstand Publishing for patiently answering all my questions and giving me wonderful advice.

Thank you, God, for giving me a second chance. I pray that what I am doing with your gift of life brings a smile to your face.

CHAPTER 1

FLYING HIGH

I did not wake up one morning, make the decision that I would grow up, live in three different states, marry three different men, seek happiness in smoke filled rooms, and wind up in a log cabin in the Adirondack Mountains. Instead, I woke up in a Canton, New York hospital the year after the end of World War II, third child of five, daughter of a dairy farmer, granddaughter of a teacher.

From the beginning, I knew I was different, I knew I could fly, I could be a cowboy, and I could climb the highest tree and run the fastest race. I remember the elation I felt racing down the steps of the big farmhouse, missing all the yellow jackets gathered on the red rose bushes lining the sides of the front steps. Life was a challenge from the start, and I loved it because I always won. No bees stung me. I was too fast, too smart, and too invincible. I loved the sky, the trees, and the clouds that floated by as I lay in the wheat fields watching them morph into dragons, horses, and flowers.

Being a risk taker has its rewards, and consequences. My father did not take kindly to a girl standing on her shoulders with her head in the register hole to the furnace. Instead, he took me by the seat of my pants and spanked me until I knew not to do that again and sent me searching for the next thing to tackle that gave me what I did not know at eight years old was an adrenaline rush. The punishment for these deeds was house arrest with access to the backyard, so I did the punishment sitting outside on the lush green grass sloping down to Mom's two rows of giant multicolored petunias. It was on this lawn, while berating my mother or father for the latest injustice foisted upon me, that I discovered a miniature family living within the blades of grass. Their names ended with the syllable "see," which included Antsee, Pansee, and Mansee. These family members embodied a mother, father, grandmother, grandfather, and several children. They all behaved because I was the boss. I do not know how long this miniature family existed. I suppose they were there as long as I needed them, and I needed them until D-day when my father announced that we were moving to some God forsaken place called Long Lake in the Adirondack Mountains.

"But Dad, what about my pigs, can I take them?" I could not, nor could I take my sugar maple with the horseshoe buried in the trunk where I hung by my legs, ate rhubarb dunked in sugar, and hot dogs cooked in a rock pit below its branches. I told my sugar maple all my deepest secrets and ran barefoot through the wheat fields on our beautiful farm. Now, I wandered these fields crying, remembering all my favorite times spent here including my first day of school.

CHAPTER 2

HOWARDVILLE SCHOOL

In September of 1952, I bounced out of bed, ran down to the wood furnace register to get dressed, ate my oatmeal, and raced out the door for my first day of school. I had waited my whole life to go to the Howardville schoolhouse with my brother and sister, Larry and Venita. I strutted out to the end of the driveway with them, leaving my little brother, Mike, behind. I anxiously waited for Mr. Howard, our teacher's husband, to pick us up in the big green car. Soon, I saw the car careening up the hill to our house. "He's coming. I see the car." I cried excitedly.

"We know, Gail. We all see it," my brother said dryly. We all piled into the car and soon arrived at the little white schoolhouse. I bounced out the door and immediately headed for the big teeter-totter. I stared in awe watching two boys soar high up in the sky and then sail down only to push up again and fly toward the clouds. The bell rang, and we all swarmed into the one-room building. I was anxious to meet, Katrina, the other kid in my class, but I could not stop stealing glances out the window at the magnificent seesaw. As soon as Mrs. Howard said, "Recess," I was out the door running for the teeter-totter and so was Wayne, a big sixth grade boy. I reached the long green board first and plunked myself on the grounded end of the board.

When Wayne and a couple of other boys arrived, he asked me, "What do you think you are doing?"

"I want to play on the teeter totter. Will you play with me?" I replied.

Wayne looked at his two friends, smiled and said, "Sure." He pulled the board down to his waist and hopped on. As his weight brought him to the ground, I flew high up in the air where I loved to be. When my end came down, I pushed hard with my chubby legs, sending me rocketing above the other children playing in the yard. The second time Wayne came down to the ground, he swung his legs over placing the board underneath his stomach. My mouth dropped open. I swallowed hard and thought, Oh no, he is going to jump off, but then he began to pull his end down with his body. Oh, I presumed, he is just playing, and I began to laugh as I felt myself flying back up through the air. Suddenly, without warning, Wayne slid off the board. As the board under me hit the ground, my whole body vibrated, I felt no pain, only hot fear, as I sat there, legs outstretched, screaming, and shaking. Mrs. Howard and all the children came running toward me. Wayne and his friends ran away. The only injury was the inevitable tooth through the lip (one of many throughout my rough and tumble childhood), which Mrs. Howard promptly cleaned up. Recess was over; I stopped crying, and we all went back to work, except for the criminal who had to sit in the corner of the cloakroom half the day with me glaring at him every chance I had.

Later on, I learned from my older brother that Wayne was mean and I should stay away from him. "Oh really, I said sarcastically, a warning would have been nice." On the other hand, who would have thought a little kindergarten girl would want to play on the big teeter-totter anyway. Would it have done any good if my brother had told me that before hand? Probably not, as that was to be one of my major handicaps throughout my life. I had to learn everything by myself and should anyone tell me not to do something, I had to do it to see why.

One of my why episodes happened on a fine spring day when Mrs. Howard and most of the students went outside for recess. She left three of us inside because we wanted to play a game called "Eraser on your head." The last words she said to us were, "Don't take those erasers outside." This game involved putting an eraser on your head and racing from one side of the room to the other without losing the eraser. I won several times

4

and then declared "Time out" so I could go to the bathroom. The outhouse was attached to the end of the school, and you entered it through the cloakroom.

"I bet you can't wear that eraser into the bathroom and leave it on your head the whole time without dropping it," Bobby challenged.

My immediate response was, "I bet I can."

Katrina chimed in, "But Mrs. Howard said…"

"Not to take it outside. The outhouse is not outside," I interrupted.

"It is too outside."

"Katrina, we get to it from inside." "Besides, she will never know," I chided. Katrina relented after Bobby agreed with me. Katrina was to go with me and be my witness. Once in the bathroom, I leaned over to pull my pants down, the eraser slid off my head, went through the hole, and landed in the waste below.

"Oh no, Katrina, what are we going to do now?"

"You mean what are you going to do? You did it."

"You and Bobby were in on it too. We've got to get it out of there before Mrs. Howard comes back," I replied fearfully. We ran out and told Bobby. I grabbed Mrs. Howard's pointer and the three of us raced back to the outhouse. I managed to touch it with the pointer, but I could not raise it up through the hole.

"We have to open the side door, Bobby said, there is a clean-out door that unhooks from the outside." We ran around the side of the school to the little door, but we could not get the latch up. "I'll get my cousin," Bobby whispered. His cousin, Dick, was in fifth grade.

Bobby raced to the playground and soon he and his cousin came zooming around the corner. Breathless, Dick said, "Bobby said you needed help." We told him our predicament, and he immediately started laughing. We all shushed him so

Mrs. Howard would not hear. Recess was almost over before he got the door open. Next, he fished for the eraser with the pointer, and two minutes before recess ended, he managed to slide it over far enough, so I could grab it. I ran inside, through the cloakroom back into the outhouse, pulled off some toilet paper and wiped the pointer and eraser clean. Then, I rushed back to the blackboard and placed them on the chalk tray before Mrs. Howard came in. All afternoon, the four of us smirked every time Mrs. Howard picked up the eraser or the pointer. I was elated that I got away with it.

Incredulous as it is, I did not get away with everything. Sometimes I was one-step behind where I should have been to escape discovery. For example, in second grade, I acquired a Mickey Mouse badge from a cereal box. I loved it and wore it to school every day. Picture day arrived in October. I got up, put on the dress Mom wanted me to wear, pinned on my badge, and bounded down the stairs.

As soon as Mom saw me, she said "Gail, take that Mickey Mouse badge off." "You can't wear it to school today."

"Why?"

"Because I don't want it in the picture," she replied.

"But…"

"Gail Elaine, march right upstairs and take that off." You did not argue with Mom when she used two names.

"Okay," I said sadly. I raced up the stairs, took the badge off, shoved it in my sweater sleeve, ran back down, hugged Mom, and tore out the door. Once I got to school, I proudly pinned the badge on my dress. Of course, a month later when the pictures came back, there I was with my toothless smile, pretty dress, and the big Mickey Mouse badge placed strategically on my shoulder for all to see. Mom was livid. She whacked me on my butt and sent me to my room, but later I caught her and Dad at the kitchen table looking at the picture and laughing.

I had a problem other than my mischievousness and that problem was talking. My brain would form the words and then trail them into sentences, but my mouth stayed stuck on the first word. I stuttered. I especially stuttered when I was excited or scared. Several schoolchildren mocked me when I tried to talk, and I came running home to Mom in tears. This ratcheted my mother into gear and her project became how to stop Gail from stuttering.

Each time, I struggled with a word; she would stop me and make me say it until I said the whole word. I had learned to skip over the word if I started struggling, so now she forced me to slow down and say the word. I do not know when the stuttering stopped, but I do know that I always had difficulty with speech. Later on, my sentence structure came out backwards when I was excited. For example, instead of saying, "Mom, I lost my shoe in the mud puddle again," it might come out, "Mud puddle my shoe, I lost." I learned to adjust to this defect even though I still have names for people and places that work better for me. For example, it is difficult for me to remember and say the name Cracker Barrel so it is "The Cheddar Cheese place." People get to know me and follow me, but people who don't know me, are puzzled, and the children in the Howardville school soon forgot about my speech because my mother cured me without doctors, psychologists, or money.

CHAPTER 3

THE SCOTSMAN AND THE FRENCH LADY

My mother was just 18 when she married my father, youngest of twelve kids, raised by second-generation Canadian French-speaking parents. She was about as big as a thimble with the blackest eyes and hair I ever saw. She had dark skin like many families who emigrated from parts of Canada, and though her ancestry dates back to France, I always wondered if she had Indian blood as she had the wide square face and coloring of the Canadian and Alaskan Indians. She grew up in Tupper Lake, New York, quit school in the eighth grade, and went to work at Oval Wood Dish, a factory where half of the town worked.

In 1937 and 1938, my father was working on the Tupper Lake Road in between farming with his father. He sometimes stayed in Tupper Lake at the Northland Hotel situated at the corner of Wawbeek Avenue and Broad St. This was one block down from my mother's home on Broad Street. He used to joke about how she would walk by the porch of the hotel where he was resting after work and smile at him. He thought she was the prettiest girl he had ever seen. Dad was a handsome blue-eyed blonde haired man with a shock of hair that hung over his forehead. He was over six feet tall with large muscular arms and legs. They began dating, fell in love, and married in February of 1938. My Mom spoke French and English and knew nothing about farming.

My Dad spoke English and knew nothing about the French speaking culture. He had two younger brothers, John and Roger, and both his parents were teachers. Grandpa and Grandma Huntley's ancestors were from Scotland. They were staunch Protestants who neither smoked nor drank alcohol, and they owned a large dairy farm in Crary Mills, NY.

Conversely, Grandma and Grandpa Disotell were staunch Catholics, spoke French, and were dirt poor. Grandma raised all the children while Grandpa worked in the woods. Mom went to Catholic Church school until eighth grade when she had to go to work. She grew up in a small house wedged between two other houses in what was called "French Village."

Different as they were, they were in love. When the road construction ended in 1940, my father landed a job as a sandhog, building a tunnel under the river near Springfield, Connecticut. This was a dangerous job because of the pressure amassed from the surrounding water, but it was work. It helped that my mother's brother, Dave, and his wife, Dora, had moved to Springfield earlier in the year. Dad and Mom moved into a small silver handmade trailer close to them next to the water, and on October 31, 1940, my brother, Larry, was born. When Larry was two years old, they moved back to New York State, bought the Butterfield farm in Pierrepont, New York, and two years later my sister, Venita, was born.

I arrived in 1946; right after my parents bought the Crary farm located about three miles from the Butterfield farm. My mother made butter, canned everything, grew flowers, cooked for numerous farm hands, helped during haying and milking, and kept our huge 13-room farmhouse immaculate. I remember many mornings laying on the blue carpet in the living room listening to the Lone Ranger on the radio. I was going to grow up, ride with him and Roy Rogers, shoot a gun, and gallop across the prairie with the wind in my hair. I knew this as sure as I knew the blue rug under me would be rolled up, hauled outside and beaten by one of us come spring cleaning month.

Spring-cleaning was a family ordeal. Everything had to go outside—couches, chairs, mattresses, and rugs. Each rug was hung over the clothesline and beaten with wire paddles that looked like tennis racquets. Two to four weeks were set aside every spring for this enormous task, and we all bustled around like mice, scurrying in and out of rooms. My mother deftly commandeered the whole operation. I loved it, though, because during those times, we usually ate out on a blanket on the front lawn for lunch, and cooked hot dogs on a stick under my favorite maple tree for dinner.

The blanket also appeared when we were sick. Mom believed that the greatest cure for anything was the sun, so as soon as the sun came out in spring (as long as there was no snow), anyone sick was relegated to laying on the blanket. Being sick also awarded a sunshine basket from Grandma Huntley, brimming with cookies, Grape juice, and fruit. In addition, illness brought the privilege of staying in Mom and Dad's bed downstairs. These three things were almost worth getting sick for with the exception of the time Venita and I had the German measles together.

One day my sister came down the stairs with red dots all over her neck and face. The next thing I knew, she was not going to school, and was sequestered downstairs to my parents' bedroom. Two days later, when I came down the stairs with red dots, I was sent to join my sister. Mom told us to leave the lights off; but as soon as Mom left, the one that was feeling good that day pulled the string on the light cord above the bed and began jumping up and down. The other one who was sick (as this sickness made you think you were getting well one day, and then came back at you the next day making you wonder how you ever thought you were getting better) would be groaning and telling the other sister to shut up and lay down. Soon, we would hear Mom's footsteps, the light would go off, and we would lay stick straight in the bed. This ordeal lasted for about two weeks. My mother survived.

Many nights after dinner, and on Sundays, Dad gathered us together to play baseball, hide and seek, or shoot the bow and arrow. One Sunday afternoon while my parents and nieces were outside drinking lemonade and chatting, I began playing

11

cowboys and Indians. This day, my fort was behind two bales of hay Dad had put in the middle of the lawn. Just as Bad News Burke was coming down on me, I jumped up from my hiding place, turned and began to run. At the same time, Marie, our hired housekeeper, was releasing the arrow from her bow aimed at the target on the hay bales. For a nanosecond, I saw the arrow six inches from my nose. I froze like a Popsicle. After that, I heard Mom scream. I woke up hours later with everybody looking at me. I had two black eyes and a white band-aid across the middle of my nose. The doctor said I was lucky, because if it had been anyone stronger, like my father, who had shot the arrow, I would be dead. I did not feel very lucky. I felt quite the opposite. Arrows and all, I loved life on the farm. My best friend, Gloria Gleason, and I played together when her mother and father came to visit mine. I loved running through the pasture dodging cow pods, and feeding my three pet pigs after daybreak's rooster crow. The farm was everything a little tomboy could ask for, and I roamed the pastures and fields as if I owned them.

CHAPTER 4

MOM AND LARRY ON THE FARM

I learned the art of listening and observation while still on the farm seated in the crotch of my tree, observing the goings on of my brothers and sisters far below me. During the summer, I ate my lunch in that tree, hung from my legs, talked to it, and felt like I owned the biggest trump card of all because no one dared climb as high as me. I loved being high up in a tree. I loved being alone. I cannot remember a time when I did not like being by myself. Should my best friend, Gloria, who lived three miles up the road in Pierrepont come with her mother to visit, I was happy, but I was just as happy playing by myself. There were moments when I played house or dolls with my sister, but only under her threat of telling on me for some bad deed, I had done.

I preferred pestering Larry, my oldest brother, because he had a gun and a tree house that was off limits to me, until five minutes after he left for school, and I found myself plopped in the middle of the forbidden fort. Larry was always fixing things, especially remote control airplanes, which hung in many directions all over his room. I remember erector sets, Lincoln Logs, and Chemistry Sets in his room. I remember one winter when my father took away his airplanes because his grades went down. They immediately came back up. I do not know if "Being sneaky" is in the family genes but my brother had this gift for quite some time, and I believe he inherited it from my mother.

A large Cedar tree grew all the way up to Larry's bedroom window. He soon discovered he could climb out his window, grab that tree, and swing down to the ground. Consequently, when Mom sent him to his room for punishment, he promptly escaped up the road to his friend, Russell's, house.

One bright summer day, he crawled out, grabbed a branch, and swung down landing right in front of my mother who said, "Going somewhere?" He was shocked and to this day wonders how she knew. She did that magic knowing trick many times throughout our childhood; hence, sneakiness was a Mom trait and she trumped us all.

Babysitting fell to Larry when he was twelve, which meant all of us staying up past midnight watching the Midnight Ghost Hour. My brother would usually yell right before the ghost ate the bad man so Venita and I would scream. After the show, she and I would crawl into bed together, terrified, never to tell, so we could do the whole thing again the next time. The down side was the nightmares. The upside was that Mom or Dad would come, get us, and carry us down to their bed if we had a nightmare, which was an upside except the time Dad fell down the stairs with me, hit his head, and bloodied his face. I thought he was dead, so I cried until Mom came running, picked me up and held me. Dad got up and disappeared into the bedroom while Mom yelled, "Don't ever get her when you are like that again!" I did not know what "like that" was, but I knew it was bad and it was my fault because I had a nightmare.

Making nightmares happen was my brother's specialty. I knew that was because he was born on Halloween; however, Halloween of 1950 became a nightmare for him. It was his tenth birthday and the day was warmer than most days for that time of year. Not only was this Larry's birthday, but it was the actually birthday of a new calf born in the morning down in the field. Usually when calves were born out in the field, my father brought the calf and the mother into the barn. Larry said he wanted to get this calf, but my father told him not to. He told me that he decided to go anyway just to look at the newborn. Peering over the electric fence at the calf, he thought, I can get him and bring him up to the barn. He walked over, picked up the calf, and started back toward the fence.

14

Suddenly, he heard a loud thumping noise behind him. He turned, glanced, and felt a stinging pain in his stomach as the cow gored him, picked him up, and threw him down like rag doll. The calf flew out of his hands and ran toward its mother. When he caught his breath, he started to roll toward the fence, but it was too late. She came at him again, digging her horn deep in his side, lifting him up, and throwing him down next to the fence. He felt excruciating pain and could not move. He lay there for a moment, hearing the grating of her hoofs against the ground as she pawed in anger at the dirt. Then in a flash, out of the corner of his eye, he saw her raging toward him once again, head down, aimed directly at him. He looked at the fence. Would he have time? Could he get under it? He stationed his arms flat on each side, and began to inch toward the fence, praying there was enough room for him to slide under before she got to him. He managed to squeeze under the barbed wire just before her head crashed like a rocket into the fence. He was safe, but now he had to get all the way to the house. Blood was oozing from his stomach as he dragged himself up the hill and across the lawn onto the porch of the house.

Mom and I were in the kitchen. She was cooking something and I was playing. I heard a low groan, turned and saw my brother bent over in the doorway covered in blood with part of his stomach hanging out. I could not move. My mother ran to him. My father came running through the door behind him. I had never seen so much blood, and I was terrified. Immediately, they were out the door with Larry, put him in the truck, and raced down the driveway stones spewing everywhere, as they turned right heading for Canton. I feared he would not be back. I was only four years old, but I knew from those horror shows that people with blood on them did not come back. My brother survived, I wanted to kill that cow. Dad did.

CHAPTER 5

DAD

Dad was my hero, and I wanted to be just like him. He came from a long line of Scotsmen, was raised purebred Presbyterian, son of a farmer and a teacher and hell bent on being my grandparent's solitary son to drink and create disorderly conduct. My nondrinking grandparents did not know what hit them when their oldest son hit puberty. My father was extremely intelligent, creative, strong, and stubborn. He loved nature, women, having fun and making money. He had to quit high school in his senior year because of the Depression. His father needed him to work on the farm. Then, his two younger brothers, John and Roger needed him to help pay for college, and he did. I often wonder what my father would have done if he could have gone to college. Without college, he managed to become a successful restaurateur, trapper, guide, inventor, skilled artisan, builder, logger, maker of maple syrup, and voracious book reader. With tremendous help from my mother, he provided for five children and was able to claim success in all of his endeavors.

I followed my father everywhere and did what he did. I grew strong for my age by lifting bales of hay, and carrying milk pails out to the cold-water vat. In the spring, the children helped Dad with plowing by riding on the rock skid hooked to the tractor. We would jump off, throw rocks on it, and jump back on eventually clearing the field for planting. Many evenings after work, much to mother's chagrin, Dad would destroy the living room by making forts out of the couch cushions for us kids.

One spring day, Dad let us go with him to the milk factory in Canton. On the way home, he stopped at a store to get fishhooks. My sister, brother, and I looked longingly at the giant ice cream cone perched precariously on top of the little building. Then, we saw Dad coming out the door with ice cream cones in his hand. We squealed in delight as he handed us our fishhooks. It was not even a store. It was a custard stand. From then on, our secret word for ice cream cones was fishhooks.

In winter, he made us igloos by squaring off blocks of snow with the snow shovel and pouring water over them. He placed the blocks on top of each other forming the rounded igloo. Then, he sprayed water over the entire form. The igloos lasted most of the winter. Throughout the winter, Dad and Mom went sliding with us in the pasture across the road. Sometimes we slid into the night or on Sunday afternoons. Dad built a beautiful red sleigh for our Shetland pony and he whisked off in the sleigh many Sunday afternoons stopping by to say, "Hello," to the neighbors. Sometimes he would hitch up, Babe, our old horse to the hay wagon, and we would ride to Grandpa and Grandma's house where they were waiting with hot cocoa and cookies.

My Dad's youngest brother, Roger, made us laugh. He had a fake tooth in front, which he could force out with his tongue. It scared us, so we would beg him to do it again, and scream with delight when he did it.

Once, Uncle Roger told me not to eat the hole in the donut. I questioned, "But why?"

He said, "Because bad things will happen." Consequently, I would leave a thin line around the hole of the donut, never biting through that line. Mom found rings of donuts everywhere, and try as she might to explain to me that I could eat the whole thing, I refused until I was old enough to know Uncle Roger was joking.

I loved the smell of our dairy farm, the sounds of the crowing rooster and mooing cows, and feeling the softness of the grass underneath my bare feet as I ran though the yard. I loved the wind in the winter and spring. I embraced it with my pudgy

18

arms outstretched as it whipped me across the front lawn from the elm tree to the big blue barn. I yelled into the wind, "I am never going to leave this place!" "No one can make me." Two months later, my Dad pulled me kicking and screaming off my beloved farm straight into a place called the Adirondack Mountains.

CHAPTER 6

SUMMER IN ROBIN WOOD

I was nine years old when everyone except me moved to the new place. My father bought a restaurant business called Lakeside Lodge in Long Lake, NY, but I went to my favorite Aunt Doe and Uncle Dave Disotells' house in Tupper Lake, NY for what I thought might be forever, but turned out to be one month. I loved that time with them and my Uncle John, who was a caretaker of a massive park between Long Lake and Tupper Lake called Robin Wood. I called it Robin Hood since that was my favorite story. I loved the idea and excitement of Robin Hood breaking the law to help the underdog.

Robin Wood was actually a small train station in Nehasane Park built in the 1890s by Dr. William Seward Webb. In 1893, Dr. Webb bought a large portion of land on the shores of Lake Lila. He called it Nehasane Park (Ne-Ha-Sa-Ne is an Indian term meaning "beaver crossing river on log) and built a massive lodge named Nahasane Lodge. It was a private park and game preserve, and during those years, any reputable sportsman could obtain a free permit to hunt and fish on certain portions of the preserve as long as they observed game laws, park rules, and fire prevention measures. At one time, a portion of the park was fenced in and stocked with big game, such as moose. That experiment ended when forest fires burned the fence; however, in spite of hunting, fishing, burned fences, and moose hunting, there was a problem—there was no railroad travel to this remote outpost in the Adirondacks.

The story goes that in 1898 Collis P. Huntington of the Southern Pacific Railroad purchased a large camp on Raquette Lake, a town just south of Long Lake. When traveling to his camp with Dr Webb, he had to park his two railroad cars at Old

Forge and take a series of small steamers through the Fulton Chain of Lakes. On one trip, he had to ride all the way sitting on a keg of nails. The two men decided that the time had come to build a railroad that would take them to their camps. Some of their neighbors who joined them on this venture were J. Pierpont Morgan, William C. Whitney, and Harry Payne Whitney.

Ultimately, it was completed and the Adirondack Division continued to operate as long as there was a New York Central Railroad. However, passenger service ended in 1965, which was just in time for me to ride on it, where I got sick, threw up several times and to this day, remember the fun I had riding that steel monster sick and all still procrastinating moving to our home in Long Lake.

I loved my aunt and uncle because they were two of the kindest people I ever knew. Aunt Doe and Uncle Dave wanted many children, but only had one. Ironically, he turned out to be one of the meanest, most selfish men I ever knew. Despite having only one child, their house on Stetson Road was always full of neighbor children. Everybody knew that Aunt Doe was the best cook around. I still remember the smell of homemade donuts and chocolate cookies. I would walk into the kitchen, be met with hugs, then sit down at the white enamel kitchen table with Uncle Dave eager to hear his latest elephant joke. Meanwhile, Aunt Doe buzzed around the old stove, potholder in hand, interjecting her latest news while baking something that smelled sinfully sweet. Uncle Dave and I had an elephant joke contest at one time—how many elephants does it take to... Whenever we met, I had at least one new joke, and so did he. Little did I know that these two kind souls would become a stabilizing force in a young life that was about to hit head on into gale-force winds.

Grandpa & Grandma
Huntley,
Dad standing, John
on right, Roger on
Grandpa's lap

Huntley Farmhouse, 1926,
Front porch where grandma taught me about birds
& constellations.

Dad & Mom

The Farm

Me and my Mickey Mouse badge

Venita, Larry, Me

CHAPTER 7

THE NEW WORLD

In July of 1955, after everyone else moved to Long Lake, under great protest I arrived at Lakeside Lodge. I saw the beach, raced to put my bathing suit on, and knew it was going to be okay as long as I could swim, throw knives at trees, and shoot my bow and arrow in the woods. I missed my Maple tree, but soon fell in love with a giant pine on Blueberry Hill across from the Lakeside, my new home.

That summer, I met Bobbie Parker, who lived a half mile down Deerland Road from me. Her father and mother, Junior and Avis, came to our bar with their two daughters. They sat at the bar while Bobbie and Kathy sat at the table and drank cokes. Bobbie and I immediately became friends. We spent the rest of that summer together almost everyday, so by the time school started in September, I had one friend. The first day of school was frightening because I had to ride on that big yellow bus. I was so relieved when the next stop was Bobbie's house and she got on and sat with me.

. I fell in love with the white birches swaying like angels in the breeze; I fell in love with the beautiful Balsam trees spreading their aroma all over me as I climbed them caking sap into my fingers. I loved running up Sabattis Mountain and Owlshead Mountain, and I loved being away from the Lakeside where I lived because inside that building was a terror brewing that grew and reeked fear among all of us.

The first turbulence in my new life came when I realized that this huge brick building was my new school. There were fifteen students just in my fourth grade class, and all the girls wore dresses above their knee. I was shocked. My dresses were below the knee. At first, I was angry declaring I would never wear dresses that short; however, within two weeks, I was begging my mother to hem my dresses. I was different. I spoke differently, looked differently, and for the first time, hated going to school. I was neither pretty like my sister, nor smart like my brother, and I was a tomboy.

One girl at school wore the shortest skirts I ever saw, and I thought she looked down on me for the way I dressed. She had a scar on her mouth where a dog had attacked her, but everybody knew her and she wasn't afraid of anything. Her name was Gloria. She was bossy, but I liked her. I asked my Mom to cut my dresses off like Gloria's dresses. Within a month, we were friends.

I learned that up here people saying, "hey," after a sentence did not require an answer. People in Long Lake were mostly French Canadian, spoke faster than I was used to, and did not smell like cow manure. I never knew I had this smell until I went back to visit my grandparents on the farm and smelled the cow manure on everyone who lived there.

The second larger turbulence came in the night when, I woke up to loud yelling noises. At first, I thought it was somebody in the bar. One quarter of the building housed our living quarters with three bedrooms, a living room, bathroom, laundry room downstairs, and one bedroom upstairs. At the time, Venita and I shared a bedroom. I rolled over to see if she was awake. She was. "Somebody in the bar must be fighting," I said. "Did you hear it?"

"Yeah, I heard it," she whispered, "It's Dad."

"What do you mean?" I asked incredulously, "That's not Dad." I could still hear the noise. Then, I heard a grumbling voice, but I could not make out the words. The door to the hall outside our room opened. My whole body froze. Someone was coming toward our bedroom. I grabbed Venita and we lay silently as he shuffled past our bedroom door. He was mumbling something as he stumbled past the door and into the bathroom.

After a few minutes, we heard him come back. Venita and I held our breath again. He walked past our door, opened the door to the bar, and slammed it shut. "See," I whispered," it was somebody from the bar who got lost."

My sister responded, "Right," and rolled over. This was not the last time someone would lose their way and wander into our living quarters to use our bathroom. The town was so small (population of 700 in the winter) that most townspeople were like family. Many times, if the public restrooms were occupied, a customer would come in and use our bathroom. As I lay in that bed, I remembered something from the farm. I remembered tumbling down the stairs with my Father when I was just a toddler.

The next day, my Dad was up joking and kissing my Mom as usual. The episode vanished into the recesses of my mind as I discovered the joy of running through the giant Spruce and Balsam trees of my woodland playground on the other side of Blueberry Hill. Blueberry Hill was right across from the Lakeside Lodge. Looking at the hill, to the left was Jekyll and Hyde Creek. I named it this because in the spring the creek twisted, turned, and crashed down the mountain with great force creating small waterfalls as it slammed against the rocks in its path. In the summer, the stream was Hyde, mild mannered meandering around the rocks taking its time to tumble down over a fallen log.

Within the woods to the left of the creek, I found two old cement walled water vats containing numerous frogs, and layers of green moss. There was a wood bridge built by someone long since dead that held me and kept me safe within its old worn timbers. This was my world and all problems ceased upon entering this hallowed ground. I loved putting on my boots, running across the road, and tearing up the path leading to my tree house in my magical world. The sound of crisp autumn leaves under my boots, trails of chimney smoke in the air, and the smell of sap from the Balsam tree became Heaven to me. It was here I honed my knife throwing, hatchet throwing, and archery skills. I relished the solidarity and not needing anyone or anything save for the smells and sounds of the Adirondack woods, until the headaches came.

Lakeside Lodge

The author and Bobbie in front of Blueberry
Hill

CHAPTER 8

BRAIN TUMOR

The headaches began in fourth grade. First, my sister noticed that my right eye sometimes moved inward toward my nose. She told Mom who immediately looked at me, but that time, my eye was straight. Venita kept insisting that it was happening, but each time Mom checked, it remained straight. Weeks went by, and I began to have headaches; however, since I knew that complaining landed you inside, I remained silent about it in front of Mom. The pain sometimes felt like a hot bullet shooting across the inside of my eyes. I dealt with it by yelling at the sky and throwing rocks at the trees until one day I landed in front of my mother who was staring at my face. She held my face between her hands and said, "Gail, look at me." I did and then she said, "Oh my God, your eye is crooked." At that moment, I knew the lying was over, so I answered all her questions about the pain and nausea, and just as I had predicted, I was sent to prison inside the house. Then, the next day she dragged me into Dr. Lazars office in Newcomb. He was our only doctor and was older than the big oak tree outside his office window. Here is where I first heard the word, "brain tumor." I was not surprised since I suspected all along that I was mentally deranged. I knew because I did stupid things like put my head down the furnace register and shoot my thumb with a new bb gun that I thought would shoot the same as an old one. I figured I was born stupid and then it was reinforced by the winds around me.

Eventually my brain tumor, Dad, Mom, and I began making trips to Glen Falls to a specialist who stuck me inside now all the time with no school and little blue pills. This doctor issued me sunglasses and once again, I heard the word "brain tumor" always in a whisper by friends of my parents. The good news was that I missed many months of school. The bad news was that when I went back to school, my crossed eye donned a patch. Once the doctor removed the patch, I wore lovely sunglasses, and finally, prescription glasses that I hated from the first day. Once again I was sentenced to inside after school. I had to take a nap after school, and then watch all the kids outside playing the games I used to play. At times, I was so tired I did not care. On other days, I wanted to play too. My eye eventually uncrossed except when I was tired. The glasses made me nearsighted, though, and since I played sports, I continually heard, "You broke them again!" from my parents. The brain tumor was eventually forgotten, healed by some miracle they said, and I continued fearlessly barreling through life at break neck speeds.

Mike

Larry

Sheryl

Venita

CHAPTER 9

LOST

Fear did arrive one hot June day in my eleventh year when I became lost in the woods on Owls Head Mountain. My brother, Larry, his girlfriend, Betty, and I decided to climb the mountain to see our friends, Pete and Elsie Jensen who were caretakers on the mountain. They were friends of my parents and I had been up and down the mountain many times with them. Pete and Elsie survived the Adirondack winters by consuming enormous amounts of whiskey and then going on the wagon in the summer to be firewatchers at the Owls Head fire tower. Pete was from Denmark and had a thick accent. Elsie had red hair and kind gentle eyes. They became part of our family and there were many summer nights spent with them on the mountain. Even at eleven years old, I loved being in the woods where no people lived. I had no fear because I knew how to read a compass. My father taught me how to find trails by looking for cuttings on trees, following a creek south, or searching for electric or telephone lines.

In the afternoon, we began our trek down the mountain; I ran ahead of Larry and Betty, waiting for them to catch up, and then spurting out again. Running fast down the smooth trail, I began looking up at the trees and the sky feeling the wind blow through my hair. I loved the smells of the rotting wood of the Adirondack forest ravaged by the "Big Blowdown of 1950"; and on this day, at this time, I was flying, I was happy, I was a gale blowing through my beloved Adirondacks.

Then, I was lost. A moment of reality rocketed in as I was racing down the mountain. At this moment, I stopped, looked around, and knew that I was not on the main trail. I ran back the way I thought I came, but every trail came to a dead end. I could not believe I was lost. I never got lost. I played everyday in the forest across the road from my house, and I was never lost. Hence, I knew I was not lost. I ran down one trail and saw a big red pine and I thought, I remember that red pine, so I know I am back on the trail, but that was a different red pine tree. Dusk was setting in and the forest was beginning to darken. I heard an animal running, a large animal, and thought, what if it's a bear with cubs, or a hungry wolf.

I did not know this forest like the one on Mt. Sabattis. Panic began to set in as I realized I actually could be lost. Then the thought entered my brain, what would Dad do? He was a guide. What did he tell me to do if I ever got lost? I began to remember my teachings, the teachings of all Adirondacker's from the time they are toddlers—stay where you are if you are lost. However, I reasoned, I know the woods, so I cannot get lost, and I continued running down dead end trails that led to nowhere.

As the shadows in the woods darkened, fear seared through me creating images of rabid coyotes and wolves just around the next bend. At about the time the wolf was sinking his incisors into my neck, I had an epiphany-- I am lost. I sat down right where I was, took a breath, and cried. I had no compass because I didn't need it on this trail, I thought. I couldn't get lost on this well-traveled trail. I began to sift through my knowledge on being lost—stay where you are; too late, follow a stream; no stream, look up for telephone or electric lines. Bingo. There it was. There was a telephone in the tower! I stood up and began running again, but now, instead of running and looking down so I wouldn't stumble, I began to look up for lines. Suddenly, I saw the loveliest sight in all the world-- a black wire. I ran toward it and it led me out to the main trail lined with telephone poles. "Thank you, Dad," I screamed into the darkening sky.

By the time I reached the bottom, it was almost dark. Larry and Betty had been searching and yelling for me, but I had not heard them due to the density of this magnificent forest. The Adirondack forest is heavy laden with Balsam, Spruce, and Cedar trees, which make wonderful wind and sound barriers. They also create visual shields along with large oaks, maples, birch, and elm trees stacked on top of each other as high as one can see, created when the Adirondack trees fought the war of 1950, and lost. The hurricane force winds were no match for the great trees rooted in the shallow soil of the rocky Adirondacks, what scientists call "New" soil formed from the Ice Age 10,000 years ago. Had it not been for this icy phenomenon, the Adirondack Mountains would have equaled the height of the Himalayas. Therefore, being lost in the Adirondacks is serious business and on that day, I learned a little piece of humility.

I soon learned how lucky I was, as every year; some poor soul became lost in the woods and was never heard from again. In 1963, a middle-aged woman was gathering mushrooms and she did not come home that night. She became the focus of a massive search that affected the whole town. The boys in my class were gleaned from school to join in the search. They brought helicopters and every search and rescue team available into the small town.

The area where Mrs. Kozier became lost was on the opposite side of Owlshead Mountain where I had been lost. It was in the fall and the temperatures dropped dangerously low during the second night. By the third night, we all thought but did not speak about the inevitable. We knew that three nights in these woods usually meant death. This woman wore a thin sweater, light slacks, and dress shoes with small heels. She was not from around the Adirondacks, so her chances of survival were grim. Dogs were brought in the second night, but on this night, it rained, so much of her scent was eliminated. This hunt was on all of our minds. Every morning, I woke up and asked whether they had found her. Nobody had heard from or seen a trace of her in nearly 36 hours. Danger lurked everywhere in this forest. We knew she could be dead of hyperthermia, a fall, drowned in Owlshead Pond, attacked by bears or bobcats, or just sheer exhaustion if she kept moving.

On the third day, an Army National Guard pilot spotted her. He was Captain Stephen Frodham, Jr. and was doing routine training flights in a small plane. He landed his plane on Tom Bissell's land on the Endion Road just beneath Owlshead Mountain and met with Percy Stanton the conservation officer who headed a search party into an old mill in the vicinity. It took many men and much effort to get her out. She was alive but could barely walk. They made a makeshift stretcher and carried her up a steep hillside. It was a difficult climb due to the old leaves, sticks, and loose stone under foot. The ambulance met them and transported her and her husband to the hospital in Tupper Lake twenty-two miles away. I remember the overwhelming relief I felt that she was alive. Later, we learned that she was a feisty 110 lb woman. Everyone said she saved herself by finding a piece of plastic and using it as a buffer against the cold and rain. She ate the mushrooms she picked and drank water from the pond. She told about the second night visit of a bear and her cub and the third night being stalked and watched by gathering Bobcats. She banged a stick on the ground to keep them away.

When I heard her account of the animal visits, I realized that those sounds I heard in the woods when I was lost might have been a coyote or a bear; but this did not stop me from continuing to tear through the woods never looking sideways or backwards for any lurking animals. I did encounter a bobcat up a pine tree once. I was half way up the tree when I looked up and locked eyes with the large cat staring straight down at me. I practically slid down the tree and from then on, I looked first, then climbed.

CHAPTER 10

TOM BOY

I thrived on dares. One day a boy named Danny dared me to jump off the roof of the house across the road from the where I lived. Danny was like a little brother to me, but he was a bully and I did not like him hurting my friends. In the winter, when the snow banks were eight feet high, it was easy to jump off this roof; however, this was spring and the roof was probably fifteen to twenty feet above grassy ground. I looked at the distance with dismay, and then I looked at the black-haired boy grinning at me as we stood on that roof. He was telling me that if I went first, he would go next. I was reluctant until he said those three words that always sent any semblance of common sense sailing out into space. He said, "You're a chicken."

I did not argue nor give him the chance to repeat those words. Instead, I jumped. I watched the ground come racing up to my feet. I hit full force on my feet, and felt excruciating pain vibrate up through my feet and into my legs. I thought my whole body would explode, and I wanted to scream at the top of my lungs. Instead, I forced the shaking to stop, stood up, smiled at Danny and said, "Come on, it was nothing." Try as he might, this boy just could not do it no matter how many times I called him chicken, wimp, and any other name that came into my head as I spat out the pain. He walked away with his head down. I walked away with a trump card that stopped that boy from hurting my friends for years.

This competitive attitude led me into any sport I could play. I liked to win. I was in every girls sport in school. After school was football with the boys and honing up on bow and arrow shooting. After my bout with the almost brain tumor, my personality began to open up like a flower. Mischievousness fit me like a glove. I was tough and liked the edge of trouble; however, I was a protector of the underdog, which included any girl or boy being bullied. Being the protector came naturally, showing up first when I was three years old and my brother, Michael, was born.

CHAPTER 11

LOSING BABY MICHAEL

I lost my little brother on October 12, 1949 while we were on the farm. Throngs of relatives had gathered at the house to welcome my mother and the new baby. My three-year-old mind, had reasoned that this baby would look like a doll. That is what Mom told me. I hated dolls. Mom got me one every year for Christmas, and I promptly gave it to my sister or drowned it in the sink. I wanted guitars, guns, and boots. I wondered if this doll would be better. I never saw a boy doll.

I heard the car tires grating on the driveway stones while waiting in the dining room with all the relatives. These adults all loomed above me and I jumped, stood on tips toes, and tried to see what was in the white box my Dad had cradled in his arms as he lumbered through the kitchen door. He put the box on the dining room table, and I heard cooing sounds coming from several people. "Oh, look at all that hair. Yes and it is so dark." I wanted to see too. I scampered around in-between legs trying to get a peek.

Finally, the adults broke away, and I was alone with the white box. I stood on tiptoes and peered over the rim of the box and there in the center surrounded by white blankets lay the tiniest baby with jet-black curls all over his head. In an instant without warning, I felt immense warmth permeate up through my feet all the way to my heart. I fell in love at that moment with this little doll. I reached out and touched his soft cheek with my index finger. At three years old, I knew I was to protect this little gift; a bond formed, cemented, and sealed in my body forever.

That afternoon, once again I peered over the edge of the white box. To my horror, the doll was gone. I panicked. I ran around frantically trying to ask the adults who were all huddled in the kitchen, but I was too little. They could not hear me. A great fear seared through me and I thought, I am not a good enough protector, because someone took my brother back. By now, I was crying and my mother saw me. She bent down and asked me what was wrong.

"Michael," I whimpered as I grabbed my mother's hand and led her to the empty bassinet. "He's gone." I cried.

"No, he isn't," my mother said softly, daddy has him out in the yard."

Author, Venita, Mike

I tore away from her, dashed outside as fast as my chubby legs would carry me. I scanned the yard, and there was Daddy with something white in his arms. I flew over to him, pulled on his pant leg and yelled, "Daddy, Daddy, let me see!" He bent over and there he was, my beautiful little brother. I could breathe. He was safe.

Another victim who needed protecting was Linda Robinson. The Robinson family lived two miles from our farm, and they were friends of my parents. Their oldest son, Allen, soon became my archenemy because he terrorized his little sister, Linda. Several couples throughout the Pierrepont village would get together and play cards at each other's house. One Friday night it would be our house, the next, the Robinsons, and so on. Linda was two years younger than her brother was, a tiny girl with beautiful blonde curls. One day, she told me that Allan always hit her and pulled her hair. He did all these things out of his parents' sight and told her he would hit her more if she told. I assured her that I would protect her, so the next time they came down to the farm, I got Allan on the ground, sat on him until he said "Uncle," and told him if he ever touched Linda again, I would beat him up.

After that episode, things went smoothly for about three months; however, one day, when we were visiting her house, she told me that Allan had strangled her pet kitten. Miraculously, it lived because her mother heard Linda screaming and made Allen release the kitten. It made me angry and as soon as I saw him, I ran up to him and pushed him down on the ground. He started screaming, "I didn't touch her! You said you would hit me if I touched her, and I didn't!"

"You tried to kill her cat, you little weasel!" I yelled back as I sat on him.

"But I didn't hit her."

Finally, I let him up without a bloody lip because; it was true; he had not touched her. However, it was not long before he was at it again. They were visiting us on a summer day when no wheat stalks moved in the stifling heat. He got mad at Linda, and I saw him hit her. Immediately, she began to scream and immediately I was on him, pushing him down, sitting on his chest holding his arms above his head. I let go of one arm and punched him in the nose. He began to cry as blood gushed out from his nose. He screamed, "I'm telling, I'm telling!"

I stared straight into his frightened brown eyes and said, "You tell and next time, I'll knock your teeth out." You hit Linda or do anything to her cat, and I will hit you again." Now say uncle and I will let you up." While his mother was putting a cold rag on his nose, he was telling her how he fell out of the tree. I stood within five feet of him daring him with a threatening stare to tell. He did not. From that day on, his sister lived in peace.

I always knew, I was strong and stupid, so, I became a defender. Did I inherit this force? I do not know, but I do know that from the age of consciousness until ten years old, my father was my great protector. I knew he would save me as I would save Linda, and I knew that he would always be there. I knew this with the wisdom of a child that creates imaginary friends, has no fear of heights, and knows that God is the Supreme Being and the Catholic Church is the only church; however, secretly, I knew that my father was God. It says in the Bible, God is the Father, and the Bible trumps all.

CHAPTER 12

HONOR THY FATHER

It is in 1957 at eleven years old that I learn about truth being ugly. Ugly comes in the middle of the night when my drunk Dad throws off my blankets and yanks me out of bed.

It is 4:00 AM. I am terrified, and for the first time I know I am neither strong nor brave. He snorts and mumbles, staring vacantly at me with red eyes. He sucks away my courage as he traps me in my room for an endless violent night that leaves me shaking. He orders me to sit on my bed in my freezing bedroom upstairs above the dance hall. He bellows, "Do you love me?" I cry and then feel the stinging singe against my right cheek as he slaps me. My chest is heaving. I am trying to say yes because I know yes is the right answer. I am shaking so violently that no words come. "Answer me he slurs, answer me, what are you stupid?"

"Yes," I squeak out in between loud sobs.

"Yes, you love me or yes you're stupid?" I nod my head right to left. By now, my whole body is shaking violently. "You love me right now?" I nod. "Say it then, say it," he hisses.

"I love you." Three little words etch out of the tiny hole in my throat. I am thinking, who is this man. This is not my father. I must be having a nightmare. Next, come more trick questions, the ones he uses to rationalize hard hands in the middle of the night. "You're lying." He hits me again. I feel the searing heat blasting through my cheek. I am wracked with sobs and cannot talk." You don't love me, say it, say it," he bellows. His bloated face looks like a rotting pumpkin. His lower lip juts out and hangs. Drool forms on his lip and drizzles down his chin. I frantically search my brain for the right answer, the one that blocks the blow. I whisper, "Please, Dad, please stop." Tears come in avalanches. Courage has escaped.

He stands up, "Thought so," he slurs and stumbles out of my room. Alone in the dark I sit staring, listening as only the beaten can listen, waiting, to hear his bedroom door shut so I can breathe.

The next day begins the silent cereal ritual--Larry, Venita and I eat our breakfast in silence. My mother stays in the kitchen preparing breakfast for the restaurant customers. I do not know how I know not to talk about last night, but I do. Perhaps it is innate knowledge, because I knew from the first time. As soon as we are out the door, Venita asked me what happened. She heard him while laying in scared silence in her bed below. Neither of us mentioned the question in both of our minds. Where was she?

As I grew older, I understood why my mother could not protect us. She was no match for my father and alcohol was steadily changing him to the point that my mother feared for her life. When the hangovers subsided, and he came out into the kitchen, cup of coffee in hand, all was supposed to be normal. Soon, I would expect him to be my Dad again, and I would start to breathe again, until the next time.

It only took a few next times for me to know that no mother was going to protect me. Instead, I turned to the woods. I ran wild between the balsam and birch; I built tree houses, and breathed the fresh mountain air, and I knew I was safe here. Many days, buried in balsams, I dreamed of protecting myself the next time he came. Next time, I will drive my knife through his heart I say with great conviction to Mike or Venita. Instead, I buried it in the big oak and cowered in a corner on those terrifying nights.

Though my concept of right and wrong was sorely damaged by trying to apply the Ten Commandments to my home life, I did know that killing someone was wrong. Hence, I chose soaring around every inch of Sabattis Mountain yelling like a wild dog. I knew where the creek bent at almost a 90-degree right angle, I knew what trees to climb so high that no one could see me; I became a feral child in the day and a domestic child in the night. My mother had no idea what was going on inside me. One time she told me, "Gail, I did not worry about you as much as the others because you always seemed happy and well-balanced." The truth was the exact opposite-- I was a chameleon adapting quite well to invisibility. By now, I could memorize all the information on God the nuns threw at me in Catechism class. I knew the answers and won rosaries, little Missals and other Catholic gifts in those insufferable contests. However, I knew God did not protect me, and I owed him no allegiance, so I did not kill my father, out of fear of burning in Hell; I did not kill him out of fear of him not dying and coming back for me. Fear can be a good thing.

Ironically, my gentle sister and brother fought back and tried to protect us. My brother, Larry, took the brunt of the abuse when he was home but at seventeen years old after my father tried to kill him by hitting him over the head with a ripped off table leg, he was sent to my grandparents to live. He was so young and so brave. I always remember this young boy trying to take on the responsibility of a parent. I remember him steering Dad away from Mom and the rest of us slamming full force into Dad's drunken fury. I was glad he got away to Grandma's even though I missed him.

The other brave person in this alcoholic home was my sister, Venita. Another evening at the homestead when my father was intent on killing my mother, Venita stepped in. This time he was beating my Mom in the bedroom. She was on the floor covered in blood. He took a break for some reason, and went into the bar. Venita and I snuck in the bedroom, picked her up, and carried her into the middle bedroom. I ran to get a washcloth to stop the blood. I was wiping the blood off her face, when I heard the door open. "Oh my God, Venita, he's coming back." I began to tremble even more, trying to calm my hands, so I could tend to Mom's face.

My sister met him just as he was approaching the bed, pushed him as hard as she could and shouted," Leave her alone and get out of here!" She pushed him so hard his elbow went into the wall. Amazingly, he staggered off to bed. That hole in the wall was there for a long time and remained a symbol of my sister's bravery.

Throughout the years, Venita became the mother of a family of four while my mother tried to survive in her own Hell. My father was what they call a binge drinker. He would go months without taking a drink, and then one day, I would get off the school bus, glance through the bar window, and see him slouched on the stool and know that Hell was back. I became extremely observant, able to see him yards away, and know immediately that he was drinking. My first response was to dash to my bedroom, to make sure the room was clean, and then sneak off into the woods. Many times I saw him sitting at the kitchen table conjuring up a reason to beat on somebody, so anything out of place in your room was a given. A later incident showed me that it did not matter if the room was clean or not. He chose his victims randomly without reason, so no one could prepare for these attacks.

On one of these binges, Venita and I get off the bus, see he is drunk, run to our room, and make sure it is clean. Later, as we are getting ready for bed, we hear his footsteps on the stairs. Terror sets in. We hug each other for the little bit of strength it gives us. My sister who is a slip of a girl runs, slams the door shut, and locks it. He continues up the stairs, and promptly kicks the door in as if it is paper. He immediately starts yelling about us having a dirty room, takes one big arm, and swipes everything off the dresser. A glass of water hits me in the chest, which I barely feel because terror trumps pain. He begins to open all of our drawers and eventually has everything in the room in piles on our floor. Before he leaves, he instructs us to clean up our room because it is a mess.

Escaping to another house was not always the solution either, though Mom used to try to get us out to stay overnight with a friend if she could. One time Venita hid out at her friend, Diane's, house. That night she was humiliated when Dad came banging on their door at 2:00 AM demanding that they release his daughter. She had to come home knowing that this was her target night.

In another incident on a sunny April day in 1954, Mom relegated Venita as babysitter of my little brother, Michael, because she was in the hospital giving birth to my sister, Sheryl. Michael wanted to walk downtown with a younger friend, but my sister knew my mother did not allow him to do that. He was nine years old and walking downtown meant walking on a busy highway. Venita and I knew that when Dad was drunk you stayed away, you hid, and you did not tell him anything. My brother had not learned this yet. He went into the bar and told my father he wanted to walk downtown and Venita would not let him. The first thing that happened was that Mike flew into the dining and told Venita that Dad said he could go downtown. We both looked at each other. I said, "What, you went and asked Dad?"

"Yes, and he said I could go so see you can't tell me what to do!"

He disappears out the dining room door just as Dad comes lumbering around the corner of the dining room looking like a raging buffalo. He heads straight for Venita, yelling that he is the boss. He hits her so hard with the back of his hand that she flips over one of the dining room tables crashing to the floor on her back. My brain races like a siren, having to make split second decisions on how to survive. While he is hurting Venita, I am hiding behind the kitchen door praying he does not find me...

51

He looks down at her, calls her a bitch, and staggers back to the bar to drink some more. Prayer worked that time. It spared me, but it did not work for my sister.

Seeing that he was gone, I ran out, helped her up, saw that she was hurt and got her into the living room. Later we learned that he had fractured Venita's back. She was fifteen years old without a protector. I felt guilty for not shooting him or grabbing a kitchen knife and stabbing him. I continued to kill him in my dreams and soon began to see this way of life as normal.

My little brother, Mike, did not escape being the sacrificial victim either. Many mornings I awoke, came out to the bar, and saw this little boy with the mop in his hand, tears streaming down his face, mopping up the whole place under orders from Dad who was still drinking, staggering around in his sock feet. I would lock eyes with my brother, and have to look away because I had failed to help this little boy I had vowed to love and protect so long ago.

There was talk at one point of going to live with Aunt Doe and Uncle Dave. They had offered their home to us. Sometimes we stayed with them on weekends or vacations, and I was awed by the peace and love I felt in that home. There was no yelling, no drunkenness. There was laughter, love, and warmth. They gave us a sliver of normalcy in our otherwise defective home life. I wanted to live with them and one night after Dad passed out, Mom packed us up in the car and we drove away. I thought we were going to Aunt Doe and Uncle Dave's house. Instead, we went to Lake Placid, slept in the car and Mom bought us clothes. I believe she was close to going to her brother's to live, but two days later we ended up back home.

There were times I became angry with Mom because she did not get us out of there. I knew I would have left him in two minutes; however, I came to realize that she was from a different era. One time she told me that her name was on the restaurant deed, and he told her if she ran away, he would go to Canada and she would go to jail for not paying the bills. This frightened her. He handled the money. She had never even written a check. She grew up in the depression, had numerous sisters and brothers, so she had to go to work at thirteen years old to help feed them. My mother was a smart, self-educated woman. She knew she could not handle this business by herself, and she did not want to burden her brother and his wife with the cost of raising five kids. Therefore, feeling trapped, she returned to the only life she felt she had, even though it might kill her.

One night my father became so full of rage, he set out to kill my mother. My best friend, Bobbie, is spending the night. We hear the horrible drunken yelling and then sliding and crashing noises like furniture being moved around. Bobbie and I jump out of bed and creep over to the side of their bedroom door. We see my mother crouched in a corner, blood coming out of every orifice on her face. My father is looming over her and yelling, "I'll kill you, you bitch."

Venita creeps out of her bedroom, sees what is happening and whispers," We have to get help. I am going to run down to Joker and Eileen's cottage and get Joker." Joker and Eileen were friends who rented our cottage on the lake about 500 feet from the lodge. It is a cold January night, and Venita runs in her nightgown in the snow to get them. Bobbie is crying and, miraculously, brave transcends fear that night because I yell," Dad, stop it!" He does not. Instead, I see his fist come back one more time and smash into her face. He hits her so hard; it lifts her body off the ground. I hear her moan and know she is dead. Finally, after what seems like hours, Joker is moving the dresser blocking the door, saying, "Howard, Howard, stop it!"

Howard hears him, turns, and stares stupidly at the man in front of him. "She's a no good bitch, Joker, a no good bitch," he mumbles. Joker ushers him out of the bedroom and into the bar while Venita and I once again carry our broken mother into our bedroom and begin wiping off the blood. One eye is bulging out of its socket. Both lips have deep cuts. My mother is barely alive. I think she will die. Soon she starts coming to and all I can think of is, thank God, now we can get out of this hellhole; now she will leave the bastard.

Eileen heads for the kitchen telephone, "I'm calling the police." "You two take care of your mother."

And in the next instance, I learn where my protection goes on those dark Godless nights; I learn about the savior-- the great protector of children; I learn hard as my mother's one eye breaks open and she whispers through blood baked lips, "no police, no ambulance, I'll be all right." The great protector shelters the monster. The children sway in the wind.

We called the police anyway. My father went to jail for three days and my mother hid out in her room for a month, scared forever by a protruding eye. She would not go to the doctor and only allowed one friend in to see her. Silence is not golden but I learned it well.

This was about the time we were all going to Catechism classes and learning about God, honor thy father and mother, and love.

CHAPTER 13

FIRST LOSS, FIRST LOVE

In December 1958, Grandpa and Grandma Huntley came from Canton to Long Lake for Christmas as they had done the year before. We were all excited because Grandma always brought us gifts, cookies, and candy. Since moving, I had been to their house the summer before for vacation and sat out on the front porch of the old farmhouse with Grandma while she taught me the location of the constellations. I loved it there. At night, she and Grandpa ate chocolates and did crossword puzzles, or Grandma played the organ while we sang. The day after Christmas, they began packing up to drive back to their farm. Mike was going with them this time, and they would bring him back before school started in January. They all left with hugs and kisses and see you in a week.

That afternoon, the telephone rang. It was the police. My grandparents and brother had been in a terrible accident. According to my brother, who was riding in the back seat, the car started to slide on the icy road. Grandpa tried to maneuver it by turning the steering wheel rapidly from left to right. Next, Michael saw a big tree looming in front of the car. His next memory was standing on the road, and then Grandpa calling out Annie's name repeatedly on the way to the hospital. Grandma died at the hospital, Mike heard the doctor say he had a concussion, and a 50/50 chance of survival. Grandpa had several broken ribs.

I knew something terrible happened when I saw Dad cry. I was in the kitchen when he went to the telephone and his face looked like it had aged twenty years in those few seconds. He told us the news and then headed for Canton hospital.

It was at grandma's wake that I discovered I could not cry like everyone else. All the relatives were mulling around saying how good my grandmother looked, and I thought she looked horrible. To me, she looked white with a blue mark down the side of her face, and she looked dead. I wondered why they were all lying. I said nothing and tried desperately to raise some tears, but none came. Finally, I had to go in the bathroom, put water on my face, and come back out pretending I was crying in order to fit in with everyone else.

The physical injuries Mike sustained healed, but the internal emotional injuries took their toll and no one knew out in the middle of nowhere in that era about sending anyone to counseling. Once again, Venita noticed something wrong with his nose, just as she had noticed my crossed eye. She brought it to Mom's attention. The doctor had to rebreak his nose and he wore a cast for several months, having to return frequently to endure painful procedures each time. Sadly, he has a sharp memory and he remembered every detail of this horrendous accident. I loved him, hugged him, and told him it would be okay, but hugs and kind words could never take away what he saw, heard and felt that day.

Grandpa's injuries healed but his heart did not. He loved his Annie and her death devastated him. Physically, he healed, but he was never quite the same.

We struggled through that winter, but spring blossomed anyway, melting the snow off the roads, and filling the air with the scent of lilacs and fresh mountain rain. Hatchets and tree climbing made way for cheerleading and boy watching. My competitive nature ran rampant in softball, basketball, cheerleading, and touch football. The woods stayed. It always stayed. "

My sister was the kind of girl that boys noticed. With her tiny waist, large chest, blond hair, light skin, and feminine grace, she was on every boy's wish list. It was as if she was the exact opposite of me. I was rugged, freckled faced, tom boyish, and lacking all feminine grace. Hence, she attracted the cutest boys, and I played baseball; however, by age twelve, I was already noticing boys, and wishing I looked like my sister.

One such boy was Art Houghton. When I first saw him, he was playing basketball. I was in seventh grade, and he was a sophomore, dating my sister. I watched him race across the basketball floor, all six feet of his brown muscular body. He had thick black hair, mahogany eyes, and a round face. He looked like an adult Hiawatha and my heart stalled out every time he entered the room.

The happiest day of my thirteen-year-old life was the day Art noticed me. It was a beautiful summer day and I was visiting my friend, Andy. Andy rented a cottage by the lake from my father. He was on a two-year construction job and befriended Art. My sister had dumped Art and was dating Andy. I would pour my heart out to Andy, so he knew I had a crush on Art. One day Andy said, "Art wants me to ask you if you would like to go for a boat ride with him sometime."

At first, I was speechless. "Why, why does he want to go with me, Andy?" I knew a boy as cute as Art would never desire someone like me.

"I didn't ask him, why." "Do you want to go?"

"Oh my God, Andy, of course I want to go!" I jumped up and hugged him. He was laughing. "Oh, wow, did he say when he wanted to go?"

"He said Saturday morning. I am supposed to let him know, so I'll tell him the answer is yes. You can meet him here at the cottage."

I was ecstatic the whole rest of the week. I barely ate or slept. Soon, it was a Saturday morning. I ran out the kitchen door, turned right, raced down the steps toward the lake expecting not to see him, and there he was, standing on the dock.

He was bending over the boat, blue flannel shirt tails hanging out, sleeves rolled up revealing strong brown arms reaching out and locking the oars in place.

I ran to Andy's cottage, knocked on the door. "Oh my God, Andy, he's here, on the dock!"

"I know, Gail, I see him," he said smiling.

"Is it real? Are you telling me the truth?" I just could not believe Art wanted to spend time with me.

"It's real, sweetie," Andy said softly, "Now just relax. He'll be up to get you." Just then, the door opened. Immediately, my eyes darted to the floor. I couldn't look at him.

"Andy says you will go for a ride with me."

I am thinking, I will, of course I will, you mean, I can. "Yes," I managed. Then I blurted out, "Are you sure you want to go?"

"Yes, I'm sure, he replied confidently, come on." He put his hand on my back and led me toward the door. My back burned. I floated out the door and into the boat and then there we were, rowing across the most beautiful lake I ever saw. It was as if today was the first day I noticed how blue the lake was, and how brilliant green the leaves were on the trees surrounding the lake.

We reached the grand stonewall that stood like a fortress diagonally across from the Lakeside Lodge. It was late spring, so the owners were not in yet. Art stepped out of the boat and reached for my hand. I felt like a princess as I exited the boat. He led me to a large round rock and motioned for me to sit down. We began to talk and soon the words flowed effortlessly from his mouth about basketball, school, and family. My whole being hummed, and I began to like him even more because I understood about his confused feelings; I understood about feeling alone, and I understood about not being good enough. I understood this beautiful boy beside me, so I listened. My code of silence prevailed; my secret nightmares remained steadfast deep in my being. The water lapped deliciously against the rocks as his head slowly turned toward me. He reached out and took my hand, and my body filled with fear that played on me like a violin. I stopped breathing. I still thought that maybe he was just being nice to his ex girlfriend's kid sister, or maybe he thought this would help him get her back. Whether that was the initial reason for it or not, I exhaled and knew that this was my time, with my first love, on the edge of Long Lake breathing in the sweet Adirondack air.

Slowly, Art sat up on the rock, bent over, put his hand behind my head, and kissed me. I will never forget that moment, the joy that exploded through me, along with the apprehension of what to do. He pulled away and stared into my eyes. He was so close I could smell him. His head came down for another kiss, this one light, just his lips touching mine. Then he pulled away slowly and said, "Well, I guess we better get back."

"Ah, Yes, I have to go to work soon," I whispered barely able to speak, wondering if I did something wrong, not daring to say anything.

When we got back to the dock, he turned to me, "Gail, thank you for going with me, I had a great time." He took me in his arms and pulled me to him. I raised my face to him. We kissed, and I fell completely in love with this wild wonderful boy. I ran all the way home, called my best friend, Bobbie, and told her everything. I loved being in love. The world stopped; the fear stopped. Love trumped all.

I was still scared it was not real and that he would never speak to me again. However, it was and he did, and we were boyfriend and girlfriend for a short time. A few months later, Art started drinking, was kicked off the basketball team, quit school and my attraction to him waned. We went back together for a short time when I was fifteen, but my young heart had moved on. By this time, I was in love with another boy, so I had to tell Art I did not love him. It hurt because I knew he was good; and it hurt because I knew he was wounded like me, and it hurt because I had to watch him walk away.

CHAPTER 14

WHEN SHE WAS GOOD SHE WAS VERY VERY GOOD AND WHEN SHE WAS BAD, SHE WAS HORRID.

I was a cheerleader, lead player on any sports team, an avid poetry writer and still willing to do most anything on dare. On the other hand, I was a virgin, won all the Catechism contests, and brought any unpopular girl into my hip group. They would accept her if they wanted to be friends with me. I did not know this at the time, but I was a leader. The high school students voted me most popular kid and biggest flirt. Perhaps there were more boys than girls, who helped me win that second award.

With all of these attributes going for me, it would seem to lay the groundwork for a successful, future. However, to me, I seemed an anomaly that never fit into any category. I could lie as voraciously about something I had done, as I could fight to help a friend. I loved my father but had to say I hated him to fit into my sibling circle, and though I liked boys, I still secretly climbed trees. My vast experience of Catholicism, family abuse, competition, friendship, and sibling love had taught me that revenge was justified, honor was ambiguous, and lying was righteous if cornered. I was cornered a lot.

One Halloween, when I was fifteen, several of us were out soaping windows. In Long Lake, the teenagers soaped windows and carried out pranks such as planting an outhouse on the school lawn. We had a wonderful coach that year. He and his wife would invite us to their house and fix us hot chocolate. Mr. Becker was my favorite teacher. On this dark Halloween night, four of us snuck up to his house and began soaping windows—

some in the back, some on the sides, and Bobbie and me in the front. I reached in my right hand jacket pocket for the soap, but instead, my fingers wrapped around a tube of lipstick. I looked over to my left at Bobbie. "Hey Bobbie, no one is around on that left window." "Why don't you get that one?" Bobbie was scared to death anyway, so she was more than willing to leave the front of the house. As soon as she turned to leave, my fingers wrapped around that lipstick tube and red paint was flying across those front door windows. I was doing it, and getting away with it. I felt like I was on fire as the excitement ignited my whole body. I finished, looked around, and snuck off into the woods down behind Rockwell's Garage and out the right hand side on down to Freeman's Store.

Then, lurking in the shadows, I saw the rest of the kids streaming down Coach Becker's driveway and piling onto the sidewalk. Next, Coach came out the door, got in his car and headed down the driveway. Uh oh, I thought, he saw the lipstick. I knew he wouldn't come after us for a soap prank. He pulled the car over, parked next to the kids, and asked," Which one of you lipsticked the front of our house?" I watched, from about thirty feet away, amazed at the soft sound of his voice.

"We just used soap, Coach, honest," I heard one of the girls reply.

Coach went on. "It is one of you because I just watched you walk out the driveway. I don't mind that you soaped the windows, but someone ground lipstick into our front window and whoever did it is going to clean it up. I can't believe you did that to us with Jenny being eight months pregnant." I thought, what does that have to do with it, but I did feel the needle pricks of fear flying through my body. My thoughts centered on how the kids could have been so stupid as to walk right down his driveway and then hang out across the road for five minutes. This was a covert operation (covert means sneaky, not seen, and not walking down the sidewalk of a population 700 town with soap in your hand).

Then, I watched Sheriff Parker's car go past me and pull over next to the kids. I snuck into the recesses of the store. He got out asking if there was a problem. I could hear almost everything as it was a cold crisp night and voices echoed across the short distance. Coach explained the situation.

"Okay, the sheriff ordered, "everybody line up so I can check your pockets," and lucky for me, Joany Mazik had a tube of lipstick in her pocket.

As they put her in the sheriff's car, against the background of her pleading cries about how she didn't do it, my fingers reached down into my pocket, grasped the lipstick tube, dropped it into the sand and snow at the edge of road, and ground it into the dirt with my boot.

I experienced this surge to go beyond boundaries several more times in my life. When faced with such situations, it was as if I was a train engine zooming along the tracks with no brakes. I could not stop, once the idea was planted in my head. I loved danger, living on the edge, and, getting away with things by using my wit. Consequently, my perception of the world was already upside down with wrong winning over right whenever the need arose. Did I know that it was wrong to let my friend take the rap for the lipstick? Yes, I knew. I had that knowledge, but the thrill of the moment trumped the knowledge and the caring. I already knew about "Not telling." I knew about protecting myself because nobody else would, and I did that skillfully and without remorse. These paradoxical qualities or defects thrust me forward, riding through life on a high-powered bike with a blown tire.

CHAPTER 15

HIDDEN ROOMS AND DUSTY BOTTLES

I cracked puberty and a can of beer one Saturday afternoon at the close of my twelfth birthday. Venita called me into her bedroom and said, "Look what I have," as she pulled out six bottles of Genesee beer from under her bed. The only interest these brown bottles peaked in me was that we were forbidden to drink them until we were eighteen. Forbidden was a big draw for me, so I immediately popped the cap off with the opener, lifted the bottle up to my mouth, and took a sip

"Ugh, this stuff is horrible," I choked as I took the bottle away from my mouth and looked at my sister. It was so bitter that it took my breath away, but when it reached my stomach, euphoria began to emanate upward; so euphoric, that it called for another sip to take the bitterness away. Four empty bottles later, the bitterness disappeared along with the nagging fears that plagued me from morning until night. This amber-colored liquid erased images of bloodshot eyes, and beds flipped over in the night. After the four bottles, I began to wonder, how many sips it took to banish the fear. Next time, I thought, I will pay attention, so I know exactly how much I will need. I fell in love in that room that night with this wonderful elixir that erased the forebodings in my heart. My sister drank one bottle and went off on a date. I stayed home, called Art at the Waukesha Bar, made an ass out of myself by telling him I loved him, passed out, and woke up looking for more.

A pattern began—Dad drank because he had to, Mom drank to soften the blows, and I drank to be me. With alcohol, my brave, smart, pretty self could march up to my drunk Dad, sit on the barstool next to him, laugh with him, and talk to him. However, without my new protector, the next time Dad was drunk, I reverted to the same scared, shaky, horrified little girl hiding under her bed in the dark.

Soon, I learned from my older brother, Larry, how to pry a loose board out from the basement wall underneath the kitchen allowing me access to the liquor cellar.

The basement of the Lakeside was a maze of secret rooms and exits beneath the floor. The door to the rental rooms was on the left side of the building. It led to a hallway and on the left was room one and two; room three was straight-ahead. Midway on the right side of the hall was a bathroom. To the left of the bathroom was a space heater. Squeezing past the space heater put you in the hallway leading to room four, which was at the end on the left .This room was only partially finished and had pipes in the ceiling. There was a white painted plank door going out of room four into room five, which was also unfinished. From this room you went through another door that took you out to an old purported Speakeasy room on the right, or you could turn left and exit to the outside. Hence, one could get out through the kitchen basement door, the liquor cellar door with a cutout door in the floor, the door leading into the bar which had been screwed shut, or through room five and out the south side of the building.

My bedroom was upstairs, freezing in the winter and just right in the summer. Bobbie, Gloria, and I smoked our first cigarettes out on the roof below the bedroom window. We shared our deepest secrets and learned to blow smoke rings on that roof. I lived in that room by choice because even as a young girl, I liked being alone. When Larry left at age seventeen, I claimed the room and wore socks to bed in the winter, so I would not have to step on the cold floor. Many winter mornings, I could see my breath, but I did not care, as long as my room was away from everyone else. At one time, Mom put Mike and then Sheryl in the small room just at the left of the stairs before my room, and at one point Venita and I shared that room, but most of the time, I hung out up there by myself writing poetry, listening to music, and dreaming of some new love, like Skip Magee. He was a million years older than me, looked like Elvis Presley and tended bar for my dad. Many nights, I snuck out of my bedroom, sat at the end stool in the bar just to gaze at him and dream about how he would ask me out, we would kiss, and he would sweep me away on his white horse.

My thrill came when one night he asked me to go to the dump to see the bears with him. It was 3:00 AM. I was thirteen and ecstatic. I waited all night even though I thought he wouldn't go, but he did, and when we returned, he kissed me on the cheek. I didn't wash that cheek for days. It was the highlight of my young life and I told all my friends. A couple of months later, Skip and Charlie Mazik had a terrible accident. They were partying one night and drove off the Long Lake Bridge sustaining several injuries. I cried that night for my one-sided love. I don't know when this crush left, but I do know that this wonderful new drink helped ease it along.

Soon, I was sneaking downstairs to get booze for parties down the lake with my friends. I reasoned that I should take the dusty bottles, like Muscatel, so my father would not notice them missing. We learned that if you plugged your nose and drank it, you got the effect without the taste. We were inquisitive kids, always exploring, and looking for excitement in a small town without even a movie theater. We did not need one. We stayed outside most of the time and gathered downtown or at each other's houses. We walked the streets at night and were safe because the biggest crime that happened was when Danny shot out a streetlight out with his BB gun.

CHAPTER 16

A NEW HOUSE AND A BEAR TO BOOT

During my first year of high school Ray Zihm, Danny's father, helped my father build a two-story house on Dock Road on the lake. I painted windowsills, lugged rocks and in exchange, Dad let me smoke cigarettes in front of him. I was thirteen. The dark Adirondack wood house with red shutters angled parallel with the point on the lake, so we had a view of Round Island to the north and the bridge to the south. The yard stretched down to a magnificent stonewall with steps leading to the dock. This home was a beautiful sight from the lake. There were three bedrooms and a bath upstairs, one bedroom, a bath, and laundry room downstairs, and a basement. When it was finished, Venita, Mike, Sheryl, and I moved into the house full-time. Venita and I shared the large room that looked out over the lake.

The best part about this move was that my parents stayed most nights at the restaurant, so now we were sometimes out of the direct line of fire. On the down side was that my mother had to fend for herself. My sister, Venita, was forced to be a mother at sixteen, buying groceries, planning dinners, trying to discipline a young headstrong boy, and being responsible for a toddler. Sheryl stayed at the restaurant with Mom in the daytime while we were in school, and stayed with us at night. Venita and Mike fought constantly, and I had to intervene several times. I was still stronger than Mike and feared nothing. Venita was tiny and not healthy. We were all kids trying to live in a grown up world.

At that time, Dock Road was a dirt road, with no name, and no streetlights. The bus would not take me home at night after the sports games. The bus driver dropped me off at the entrance next to the post office, and I had to walk home. Many nights, as I cautiously walked down that creepy road, I heard animals crashing and skittering through the trees. Most of the time, I ran all the way home.

One night, Bobbie and I were meandering home from Teen Club, which was held in the town hall. We rounded the corner near the Long Lake Motel, and stood face to face with a bear. The bear was in the middle of the road directly in front of us. We screamed and the bear grunted. He ran crashing through the woods, and we ran most of the three miles to the restaurant. Mom was already asleep, and we refused to walk back down that road, so we slept upstairs in my old room. When we came down to the kitchen the next morning, Mom was surprised to see us.

My bear fear was immediately overshadowed when I realized that no one knew where I was all night, and no one had looked for me. This was exciting news! It gave me free rein to sneak out many nights and run around until early morning. Bobbie and I saw many things peeking out the dining room window of the Lakeside at 3:00 AM. We saw wives in cars with other people's husbands, drunks staggering into cars and driving away, and men hitting their wives then coming to church the next morning acting pure as snow. Bobbie and I did not question this adult behavior because it was normal for us.

CHAPTER 17

SEASONS IN THE SUN AND SNOW

During those teenage summers, I worked at the restaurant. I would finish my shift, fly into my room, throw off my waitress uniform, meet my friends, and skim down the lake in my 12-horse aluminum boat full of beer, soda, chips, and us. We had many party spots on Long Lake-- Camp St Mary's Beach, Slim Point, or Turtle Beach. Sometimes, we piled into Bobby Jennings father's Chris-Craft boat and zoomed down the lake drinking tall brown bottles of Genesee or Schlitz, screaming in delight as the wind whipped through our hair. We listened to our transistor radios, swam, danced, and drank into the night. Somehow, we managed to get home safely. I would drag myself out of bed in morning vowing to stay home that night, but as soon as the sun began to fade on the horizon, there I was sixteen and ready to do it all over again.

Growing up in the Adirondacks was thrilling in the summer when the tourists all arrived in their rectangular campers and jeeps loaded with tents, canoes, and kids. We water-skied, swam, and tanned on the beach, flirting with the city boys. I zoomed around in my boat, doing circles as sharp as I could in the water until water came in the sides. My father owned a cabin cruiser and one of our favorite sports was to find a group of boy scouts canoeing down the lake and circle them until they tipped over. At that time, there was no lake patrol or boat registration, so sometimes we had "Ram the boat contests," or "Tip the boat over contests." We did these things because we were invincible teenagers, let loose on a lake with an engine.

One summer day, Bobbie, Gloria, and I planned a canoe trip to Turtle Beach, which was just west of the opening at the north end of Long Lake. It was approximately seven miles from my house. We packed a lunch (no beer this time) and started down the lake around ten o'clock in the morning. We chatted, paddled, and had a great time all the way down, yelling at the boys in all the camps we passed. We arrived at the beach, ate, swam, and then began paddling home in the afternoon. We covered about a mile before we discovered the leak. Bobbie began to bail us out while Gloria and I paddled, but the leak was so big, we were filling up with water faster than we could bail it out. Frantically, Bobbie and Gloria continued bailing while I struggled with the paddling. "Damn, wouldn't you know, that there is not another boat anywhere in sight," I puffed as we scanned the horizon.

Bobby chimed in, "Gail, we may have to leave the canoe and swim to shore." If you grew up in the Adirondacks, by five or six years old, you could swim. Long Lake is a narrow body of water, so no matter what your position on the lake, you could swim to shore.

"Dad will kill me if this boat sinks!" I yelled back. "Let's try to turn it and paddle to shore."

"Wait, look, Gloria pointed, I see a boat coming."

I stopped paddling, looked up, and started waving my arms. We all commenced waving our arms and shouting, "Help; Stop; Help us!" The boat did not slow down.

Oh my God, that jerk isn't going to stop!" "I can't believe it," I lamented. We began to shout even louder and stood up waving. Finally, we heard the engine crank into a low gear. "He sees us!" we all squealed at the same time. When the boat pulled alongside the canoe, we saw that it was a local man.

"Looks like you've got a problem here," he said smiling.

"We've got a problem all right; Gloria called out, can you tow us to Gail's house?"

"Sure can," he said and with great proficiency, hooked a rope onto the front of the canoe and towed us home., We never canoed that far again, though we visited Turtle Beach many times after that, loaded down with beer in a boat with a motor.

Winter season ushered in outside fun for us. We carried our skates to school draped over our shoulders; put them in our lockers, and after school raced down the path to the skating rink where we played ice games and hockey. In the winter, there were winter boys to flirt with. There was basketball, cheerleading, stolen kisses on the bus, and romantic encounters behind the last bench at the skating rink. The rink was the bomb. It was where you went to see everybody, even adults at night. I recall many beautiful snowy nights figure skating around the rink, looking up at the lights, and loving this place ringed by giant snow laden conifers. I felt safe and free as I twirled high in the icy air and sailed away backwards on one skate. I felt beautiful, strong, and fearless in the dark night illuminated by the rink lights and the circle of white snow surrounding the icy mirror in this remote fairyland.

The pond was between the spill way and the Adirondack Hotel. According to a local man, Wilbur Carey, before 1932, the pond was a swamp with a little stream of water running through it. During the depression, the government initiated the spillway project to create jobs. Wilbur worked on it. A land bridge connected Pine Island to the Sagamore Hotel and then Sagamore Hotel to Sagamore Road. The land bridge filled the swamp creating a deep pond. This pond became our skating rink. On the edge of the north side of the pond up on the spillway, the town built a small shack. We all piled into this warm wood-heated building to put on our skates. Mr. Ricky and Hank Faxon supervised the rink during this time. They kept the fire going, broke up fights, and helped us tie our skates. Some nights, when the temperature plunged far below zero, as many as twenty kids piled into that little shack getting thawed out for ten minutes, and then flying out the door and zooming onto the creaking cracking ice. During several of those years, the snack bar next door had an outdoor window. We would walk over on our skates and buy drinks and candy.

Other winter activities included building fires on the lake, and cooking hotdogs and marshmallows washed down with hot chocolate. We tobogganed down Golf Course hill and Blueberry Hill, and snowshoed through the woods. I loved my town, my school, my friends, and my woods, but I dreaded going home where sometimes, sleep came slow.

During these years, I did not work for a wage; however, tips were quite lucrative for a young girl, so I always had money. I have fond memories of summers because I spent them with my two best friends, Bobbie and Gloria. My other best friend from the farm in Canton, also named Gloria, came and stayed for a couple of weeks in the summer and the three of us were constantly chasing boys and flying down the lake in the boat.

In my later teens, my brother, Mike, became my best friend. Many times, I hid him under my bed when he came home drunk at fourteen years old while Mom looked for him. She would crack my door open and say, "Has Mike gone up to bed yet?" "Have you seen him?" He was now sleeping upstairs, and I had moved to a downstairs bedroom because Venita was in beauty school in Albany.

"Yes, I lied, I heard him go up a little while ago." She would leave and I would pull him out from under the bed. "Go, Mike, she's gone." He would sneak up the stairs and go to bed. During those years, Mike and I readily lied for each other. We shared our secrets, hopes, and dreams, drank beers in the woods, and camped out. One camping trip was to Corner Pond where Dad had a hunting camp. I decided it would be fun for us to hike in and spend a night or two. Mike was agreeable and a week later Mom dropped us off at the entrance to the trail on the Newcomb Road. We walked briskly through the woods even though Mike had broken his arm a few weeks earlier and it was in a cast. It was a ten-mile walk to the pond. From there, we launched a

74

rowboat dad kept hidden among the fiddlestick ferns. I rowed us over the pond to the dark wood camp perched on a small knoll. The air smelled dank and the only sound was the rat a tat tat of the Pileated woodpecker's beak drilling for food. We laughed, shared our thoughts, and arrived at the dock within ten minutes.

The first thing we did was scour the cupboards for food and alcohol. The second thing we did was remove the beer from our backpacks and drink one. We sat outside the cabin discussing how wonderful it was to be in the forest and away from that house. We ate lunch and waded in the water. Mike could not swim because of the cast. In the meantime, Mike found more booze in the cabinets and began to drink that. He was getting smashed and soon decided that he was going swimming. I said, "Mike, the doctor said you can't get that cast wet."

"To hell with the doctor, I'm going swimming." He got up staggering down toward the pond."

"No, Mike, I yelled as I ran after him, you can't go in."

"Watch me," he slurred, and proceeded to half walk and half fall down toward the water.

"Oh yes I can," I said as I whisked him around placing my face within inches of his. "You are not going in that water!"

"Out of my way, Gail, I'm going!" He tried to push me away, but I would not budge. Finally, he pulled his cast arm back, swung, and hit me on the side of the head with it. It stunned me, and I was livid. I pulled back my fist and hit him the mouth. He went down. I got ready for him to get back up, but he did not. He finally passed out on the edge of the pond and slept there most of the night.

The next morning on our way back, he kept saying, "I don't know why my teeth hurt." I just smiled and kept on walking. Later, when I told him about the punch in the mouth, he laughed about it, and we both put it in our good memory bag because we were in the woods together and that trumped bonks on the head and fists in the mouth.

CHAPTER 18

TOM TOMS AND REVENGE

When I was fifteen, a man named Tom Rotollo opened a new place for kids on the Tupper Lake road across from the Lake Eaton entrance. He named it Tom Toms, installed a jukebox, kitchen, and small dance floor, and made pizzas and sandwiches. Tom was an ex golden-glove boxer who was a single Dad raising a ten-year old daughter and a younger son. We all loved this man even though he was strict. Nobody rebelled against his rules because they knew he was tough, but fair. Many nights I saw him teaching the local boys a few things he knew about boxing. Night after night, we danced the Mashed Potato, the Monkey, and the Twist across that old wood floor, then piled into the booths, and flirting with our friends.

One night when I was sitting with my friends, a man came in dressed in a Navy uniform. He sat down with us and introduced himself as Stewart. I vaguely remembered him riding on my bus for a year or two when I was in elementary school before he graduated. He asked me to dance and I said no. He teased and kept asking, and I kept refusing. He was old to us, and we were all wondering why he was there. Before he left, he whispered in my ear, "I am going to marry you some day." I looked at him as if he was crazy.

"Right," I laughed and got up to dance with my boyfriend, Don. I had several boyfriends in high school, but I never seemed to love them enough to stay with them through the summer season. It was a pattern for me from the time I was old enough to like boys. In my freshman year, I dated Don Sharp. He was dating someone else, and I wanted to see if I could get him. I loved a challenge. Don was intelligent, good looking, tall, and funny. I dated him for two years but only in the winter. In June, I would invent an excuse to break up with him, so I could date the summer boys who came up to camps on the lake, such as Riverdale and Onondaga. I could perceive but not empathize with Don's feelings. I was consumed with me, what I wanted and God help those who came into my life expecting anything different. All of my Catechism teachings about God and the church centered in my intellect, not in my heart. I learned from my father that men could hurt you. I learned from being alone in the woods, that I was my own best friend and protector; I learned to hurt you before you hurt me.

Catholic classes sunk in at this level and though I was mischievous, I lived on the virgin side of church. Though my boyfriends tried valiantly to bring me to the other side, they respectfully surrendered to my rejections, except for one boy on one cold windy night. I was at Tom Tom's and it was getting late. I had to be home by ten o'clock, and I lived about five miles away. It was getting late and my curfew that night was 10:00 P.M. None of my friends with cars showed up that night, except one of the older local boys. He heard me telling Tom about my dilemma and offered to take me home. "Thanks, I said, I appreciate it."

"No problem," he replied as we walked out, got in the car, and headed down route 30.

Suddenly, he turned onto Endion Road. I said, "Where are you going, this isn't the way to the Lakeside?" The Endion Road was a well-known making out place, so I was immediately uneasy.

He answered, "Oh, I just want to take a short ride down here for a minute."

"But I need to get home now," I lamented. "I don't have time for a ride." Silently, he continued driving down the lonesome road. I grabbed the door handle. Suddenly, he pulled off the road into an abandoned driveway. He shut the engine off, and in a flash, grasped the back of my head with his hand, and leaned down to kiss me. I pushed him away, "What in the hell do you think you're doing?"

"Ah, come on Gail, you know you want to," was his reply as he continued to grope at me. For a moment, I was in shock. I could not believe this was happening.

"No, I don't. Get to hell off me." I pushed hard and tried to squeeze away from him and clutched the door handle, but he was strong and grabbed me around my arms so they were smashed straight against my sides. He kept on trying to kiss me as I moved my head back and forth feeling his saliva on my cheeks. I thought I was going to be sick. My mind raced frantically trying to figure out what to do. I was an athlete and strong for a girl, but he was a wrestler. Out of the corner of my eye, I saw the gearshift. In this car, it stuck out quite far. By now, he was practically on top of me. I said, "Let my arms go, and I will kiss you." He did. Immediately, I shoved hard against him pushing him with my hands and body .Because he was practically on all fours halfway over me, crouched away from the gearshift, when I pushed him, the handle hit him squarely in the groin. He groaned and let go of me. Instantly, I jammed the door handle down and rolled out the door like an acrobat. A thin layer of snow crusted the ground and a cool wind whipped at my face, as I started running down the old road. Soon, I saw his lights coming up behind me. I ran faster, looking into the woods contemplating my chances of losing him among the trees.

He rolled down the window and yelled, "Gail, get in the car! I'll take you home."

I screamed back, "Are you crazy? I'm not getting in the car with you and tomorrow your best friend and everybody in school is going to know just what kind of creep you really are!" I was so mad; I did not feel the snow, or the wind. I just kept walking. In the end, after walking about a mile with promises from him that he would not touch me or try anything if I kept quiet about what he did, I agreed and stepped back in the car. He took me straight home with me once again promising not to tell. I jumped out of the car, ran through the door, went straight to the telephone, called Bobbie, and told her what happened. Then, I called my boyfriend and told him. I had no allegiance to this creep and would have promised him anything to get out of his car. Two nights later, Bobbie called telling me that this boy had spread the news all over school that I let him touch me. I was furious. I immediately called my boyfriend, Don, to find out if he heard the rumor. Yes, he had, and he knew me and believed me. I was seething with resentment and hatred for this boy and immediately plotted a revenge plan. Friday night, all the local kids would be at Tom Toms. That is when I would enact my plan. I came in that night about 8:00 PM and invited many of the local boys over to Don's and my booth. I then asked Don to invite this boy over to the booth. He did. As soon as he sat down, I began peppering him with questions about that night and what really happened. "Why are you telling lies about me?" I asked.

"I'm not," he lied.

"You know, even Don knows they are lies. For Gods sake, he's my boyfriend. Everyone knows you fabricated all of this. You never touched me. You made it all up. Tell them, tell them right now." A little more of this and soon, his head was hanging down and Don was telling him to be a man and apologize to me.

He managed a low mumble, "You're right, I made it up, now leave me alone." He got up and rushed out the door without even an, "I'm sorry," because he wasn't sorry he did that to me. He was sorry he was caught though, and I felt vindicated anyway because he was at least humiliated. Revenge was my friend that night.

CHAPTER 19

HIGH SCHOOL HIGHLIGHTS AND LOWLIGHTS

Playing games with boy's hearts was exciting. When they put their arms around me, I shivered, when they looked at me and I knew they only wanted me, I laughed, and when they came back after I left them, I felt invincible.

I met a boy in eleventh grade named Phillip. I had known him all through school and knew he never dated, at least any local girls. He was in tenth grade, had black hair and a cute boyish face, and we rode the sports bus together. Don was now in college so my eyes were roaming, and they set on this boy because he was shy and unattainable. It would be a challenge to get him to date me. I began flirting with him, and before long, we were an item. I had his jacket and his class ring and when we were making out in the back seat of the car, I felt like I never wanted to stop kissing him. He lived in Whitney Park, was smart, athletic, and had a smile that melted my heart.

Despite these qualities, when June rolled around, I broke up with him and when September came, I went back with him. That is how I lived on excitement's edge. I did this every year and when the next June rolled around, I started seeing the summer boys, but I did not break up with Phillip. Being good was something I did not do well. I tried all sorts of ways to stay on the "good" track like hanging out with my Wesleyan Methodist friend who was always good and hoping goodness would come to me through osmosis. It only stuck for about two weeks, and then I would do something like throw a snowball from outside the school inside the school at the custodian and barely miss the principal by an inch. It just seemed like I was jinxed to do bad things and sometimes get caught. On the other hand, bad things tended to follow me like when two different teachers tried to molest me. One teacher was not strong, and I got away from him telling only my friends and my sister and no one else. Luckily, his class was one I could drop, and I did.

The other teacher was a well-known molester among the female school population. One day, when Gloria and I were playing ping-pong in the room next to his office, he snuck in and grabbed me from behind, cupping my breasts. I screamed, "Let me go," and struggled with him but he was strong. Gloria ran out the door and down the hall yelling for Mr. Wheeler, the shop teacher, to help. Finally, when coach heard Mr. Wheeler coming up the hall, he released me. I told Phillip and a couple of other boys and we reported it to the principal. He did not believe us, and that teacher was still there when we all graduated, molesting girls until many years later when he was caught so red handed that even the girls had to be believed.

One evening around the beginning of July, Phillip came into Tom Tom's and asked me to come outside with him. I was irritated. He lived ten miles from town and did not come to this hangout, which suited me fine because I could date the summer boys and still keep him. When we got outside, he looked me in the eyes and said, "Gail, I've met someone else." Suddenly, the irritation vanished. Fear flashed through me like a bolt of lightening.

"What do you mean, you've met someone?" I said.

"I've met another girl and we are dating."

"What?" I could not believe what I was hearing. "But, I love you, Phillip," I whined. What was the matter with me? Five minutes ago, Phillip was the last person on my mind, and now I wanted this boy standing in front of me more than I wanted anything in the world.

"Gail, you know why?" he looked at me with his head tilted slightly to the side.

I knew why, but I did not know if he knew I had been seeing other guys, so I played the game, "No, I don't," I lied. "How could you do this to me?"

"Me, I didn't start this, Gail." You've been seeing other boys since school let out."

"I have not," I snapped back.

"Well, I know you have and I want my jacket and ring back."

"So you can give it to her?"

"No, I just want it back."

As I stared into his face, I felt humiliated. Tears welled up in my eyes and I willed them back. Now, I was mad at myself. How could I have flirted with those other boys? I knew I had lost this game so I said, "Ok, Phillip, meet me here tomorrow night." "I will have your jacket and ring" I walked away shaken and hurt, and then I thought, oh well, I will get him back in the fall. Fall came, I saw Phillip once, and I knew it was over. I was shattered for eternity, which at that time spanned approximately two weeks.

Varsity Cheerleaders 1964; L to R, B Shaw, G Huntley, D Helms, E Harrington, G Boudreau, D LeBlanc

CHAPTER 20

NO BRAKES!

By now, I knew I was going to Hell anyway, so I jumped into mayhem full on. Hell was on the horizon because I had rung the Catholic Church bells at midnight one night, and no one ever knew who did it until right now. Hell awaited because I had lied and let another girl take the rap for my deed; I had stolen money daily from my parents, and when I went to confession, I made up stuff just because I couldn't tell the priest what I really did. I knew Purgatory was not even waiting for me. God did not need to put me in holding while awaiting a decision. I was guilty, knew it, and drank or flirted it away.

Sometimes I did not create the mayhem. Sometimes it appeared naked out of nowhere. When I was 16 years old and a new driver, it found me in an old 1932 pick up truck my father had restored. One day, Gloria and Bobbie were at the Lakeside and we wanted to go downtown, but Dad had the car, so we decided to take the truck. Bobbie got in the front with me, and Gloria jumped in the truck bed. I turned the key, put the long floor shift into reverse, backed out, and we were on our way. We got to the top of Len West's hill, started down, and as we picked up speed, I realized, to my horror that the brakes went all the way to the floor. "Oh my God, Bobbie, there aren't any brakes!"

"You're kidding," she retorted thinking I was kidding.

"No, I'm not kidding. See." I pushed the brakes and nothing happened.

"Oh, my God, what are we going to do?" By now, I was cresting Freeman's store hill. "Gail, we can't go down this hill!"

"Well, we're going. I can't stop it!" Tell Gloria what is going on and tell her to hold on." Bobbie yelled out the window to Gloria, and just as she got her head back in the window, I began maneuvering the truck around Freeman's Corner. "Oh no," I screamed, "Look, Bobbie!" Our mouths dropped open, and we both froze for what seemed like minutes. There wobbling across the road, cane in hand was old Mrs. Freeman. She was almost in the middle of the road and getting ready to cross the line into the right hand lane where I would be in seconds.

Gloria and Bobbie started yelling, "No brakes, No brakes!" She could not hear them, and the only way to miss her was to swing way out into Freeman's parking lot dangerously close to the store steps. I eased the wheel to the right, and swung out. It looked like my tires were inches from the steps, but I missed her. I immediately yanked the wheel to the left tires squealing on the concrete barely missing the steps. We all breathed a sigh of relief; however, it was short lived, because now we were rolling up on Becker's Hill. It was longer than the first hill, but also had a sharp curve at the bottom. Not turning at the bottom of this hill sent you straight down the boat launch into the lake. During the previous winter, I had witnessed a car missing the turn and flying straight into the lake. By now, Bobbie and Gloria were screaming and laughing at the same time. I was silent, saving all my concentration for the task— maneuvering this old truck around the corner. We gained speed on the hill; however, I managed to get it around the corner and coast into the sidewalk finally stopping at Lahey's Store.

Now, most kids would have gone to the pay phone and called their parents, but we were not most kids. I convinced Bobbie and Gloria that we would be fine on the way home because it was up hill the whole way and when I got to Green Harbor Cottages, a business about 50 feet from the Lakeside, I would turn the key off and we would roll to a stop in the parking lot. They believed me and climbed back in the truck for the ride home. On the way back, the little truck chunked along, and it was much easier to manage the speed. I never went above 25 miles an hour. We relaxed and shouted back and forth about our near miss and my driving skills. As we inched by Green Harbor, I turned the key off. The truck began to roll and roll and roll until it rolled right into the two posts holding up the awning in front of the Lakeside dining room. I hollered back to Gloria, "Get down!" We halted to a stop when the grill hit my Dad's flower boxes. I saw people jumping up from their seats in the dining room. Mom came rushing out, her face filled with fear frantically asking, "Are you all right?"

We could not answer because we were laughing so hard, we could not talk. In the meantime, my mother was getting madder and madder because she was scared, and we thought it was funny. Finally, we stopped laughing and reassured Mom that we were not hurt. Standing by Mom was Bob Hamner, a friend and regular bar customer. I looked at him and said, "Mom, if you and Bob hold each post, I can back it out a little."

"No, get out of that truck right now," she snapped back, I'll get your father and Bob to do it." As she spun around to go back through the door to get dad, he came barreling through the dining room his big frame filling the doorway. I took in a breath, held it, and waited in silence. He looked at the truck with pole on top, then he stared at me, "You do this?"

"Yes," I said meekly. "Dad, the brakes didn't work. I swear."

"Guess not," he replied and then broke out in laughter. I let my breath out and before I knew it everyone but Mom was laughing.

Mom huffed," I'm just glad you didn't get hurt. Howard, why did you let her take that old thing with no brakes anyway?" She shook her head, opened the door, and went back inside. Earlier, Dad had told me the truck was fine, and I could drive it. After they backed the truck out, Dad told me how I could have used the parking brake to stop the truck. One more life lesson blasted into my psyche by almost killing my friends, and poor old Mrs. Freeman, who never knew how close she came to the almighty end.

CHAPTER 21

THE PINE SOL CAR CAPER

Another exploit in a vehicle transpired in Venita's new car. I was sixteen years old and Bobbie, Susan Kohler, and I wanted to go drinking in Tupper Lake. I begged Venita to let us take her car to the movie theater in Tupper. Eventually, she reluctantly agreed, contingent upon me swearing we were not going to drink. I assured her we would not as I shoved the bottle of Vodka deeper into my pocket book. She magically handed me the keys. Then she said, "And I want it back by ten o'clock."

"Ten, but that is so early, I whined, how about eleven?"

"Gail, you're going to the 7:30 PM movie. It will be out by 9:30 PM, so you should be able to make it by ten."

I decided not to push it. "Okay, I'll have it here by 10:00. Thanks."

I ran out the door, jumped in the car, and drove a mile down Deerland Road to Bobbie's house to pick up her and Susan. I pulled over and beeped the horn.

Bobbie came out, "My God, Gail, I can't believe she let you have the car."

"Me neither. Get in," I said excitedly. "She thinks we're going to the movies."

"Gail, you lied to her?"

"Yup, and she believed me, so I got the car."

"Uh, Gail, I don't want to get in trouble with her, Susan remarked."

"You won't. If she finds out, she will be mad at me. Now get in so we can get going. We have to be back early."

"Okay, if you say so, but Joe heard we might go and wants to know if he can go too." This town was so small that no secret was sacred.

"Really, Bobbie, Joe?" When this boy drank, he either got sick or passed out, but we were friends, so I swung down Sagamore Road and picked him up.

In twenty minutes, we were in Tupper Lake at the Waukesha ordering drinks already on fire from swigging the bottle of Vodka on the way. Bobbie, Susan, and I drank and danced. Joe just drank. At 11:00 PM, seeing as how I was only one hour late, I told them we had to get back. By now, Joe was so drunk he could barely stumble to the car, and within five minutes, he was throwing up on the floor. He vomited all over the floor and seat and then passed out. It stunk.

"Damn it, Bobbie, I knew this would happen," I said arms in the air. "We should never have picked him up." "Venita is going to be so mad at me."

"Well, you decided to get him. All I did was tell you he called."

"Never again, I shouted!" If I ever decide to take him with us again, shoot me." "Now, how are we going to wake him up when we get him home?" "Joe, Joe, wake up," I yelled. Nothing. He did not move. We tried to arouse him when we reached his house, but no amount of screaming, poking, or slapping budged him. Finally, the three of us got out of the car, grabbed him by the feet, and pulled until we got him to the edge of the seat. Then we pulled him out by his shoulders, dragged him onto the lawn, and pulled away just as his big brother was coming out the door to see what was happening.

By the time I dropped Bobbie and Susan off and arrived home, it was almost midnight. Venita met me at the door. She was furious, stuck her hand out for the keys, and told me I would never get the car again. I was thinking, my God, she is already mad because I am late; it will be heart attack time tomorrow when she sees the inside. I knew I had to clean it up before that happened. Consequently, at 1:00 AM I began cleaning up the vomit with paper towels. Then, I dumped half a bottle of Pine

Sol all over the carpet and scrubbed it clean. When I finished, it no longer smelled like vomit; now it reeked of Pine Sol so strong it almost burned my eyes. I quickly surmised that I couldn't leave it smelling like this either. In fact, this smell was almost worse than the vomit smell, so then I poured out a bucket of water and dumped it on the floor trying to rinse the smell out. It did not work. Finally, sometime in the early morning, I gave up and went to bed. The next morning, Venita woke me up screaming about how her car smelled like a Pine Sol bottle and how she told me not to drink in this car!"

I opened my eyes and immediately lied, "I didn't.

"Liar, you did something and tried to clean it up."

"It was Joe. He got sick because he ate too much popcorn at the movies. We tried our best to clean it up, but I guess I used too much Pine Sol.

"It's horrible," she screamed, never letting on whether she believed the popcorn story. "Don't ever ask me for my car again! I never asked again until two years later when once again I was late, but this time it was because we got lost coming home from the movies.

CHAPTER 22

NEW MAN, NEW CAR

When I was seventeen years old, I met Kenneth. He came to Long Lake to work for the local gas company. He rented a room from my father and ate his meals at the restaurant. He was twenty-two years old, funny, and drank a lot of alcohol. I sat with him at the dining table nearest the kitchen while he ate and performed hilarious antics, such as putting his cigarette in his ear and blowing smoke out his mouth. He was a comedian; he made me laugh, and I needed to laugh. I began looking forward to coming home from school and sitting with my new friend. I asked him questions about boys and he told me what he thought. I was still dating Phillip, so he was our usual conversation topic.

One night, Kenneth came in all bent over holding his back. I asked him what was wrong, and he told me he had a bad back. I asked why, and he told me a terrible story about the St Regis Hotel burning to the ground. He was tending bar at that Saranac Lake hotel, went to sleep that night, and woke up smelling smoke. He jumped out of bed, opened his fifth-story window, and saw the firefighters below holding a life net. They instructed him to jump, but he began to hear yells for help in another room. He left his window, and found his way to their room by groping the walls. It was a man and his wife trapped in their room. He led them out and into his room. The woman was too scared to jump, so Kenneth and her husband had to push her out. Heroically, he told her husband to go next. By now, the flames had reached his room and were licking at Ken's clothes. Kenneth was the last one out of the hotel. His shirt was on fire when he jumped. By the time he reached the net, the flames had burned his back. In addition, he injured his back in the jump because there were not enough available men to hold the net securely. I learned that he was released from the hospital with a full back brace just before coming to Long Lake. He needed work and applied for the job. He went to work everyday, but this job involved lifting tanks on a dolly over uneven ground. Some days he wore his brace just so he could work. I admired his bravery and loved his humor, and it was not long before I developed feelings for this man, much to my parents' chagrin.They did not like that he was so much older than I was, and Dad said he had a bad feeling about him. He wondered why the lad didn't have a car, and why he came to Long Lake to work.

In June, just two days before graduation, Dad came and picked me up at school. He was driving a 1962 white Buick convertible. I came out the school door and saw Dad in the car. He motioned me to come over and get in the passenger's seat. I did and commented, "Dad, you bought a new car."

"Yes, he said, do you like it?"

"I love it, but it isn't a Chrysler like you always drive." I loved this little car. The top was down and we began pulling out of the parking lot and heading toward the restaurant. I thought it was weird that he picked me up, but figured he had just purchased the car and wanted someone to see it. We pulled into the Lakeside parking lot. We both got out. He walked over and handed me the keys.

"Congratulations, this is your graduation present," he said beaming from ear to ear.

My mouth fell open and I began to scream and jump up down. "Really, is this a joke?"

"Really," he said. "You need a car for college so this is it." "Do you like it?"

"Oh my God, oh my God, Dad, do I like it? I love it. Thank you. Thank you." I shouted as I hugged him. I looked over and Mom and Avis, Bobbie's mother, were looking out the window laughing and waving.

94

"Can I take it to Bobbie's house and show her?"

"Sure, it's yours." I jumped in the car, turned on the engine, and rolled out of that parking lot feeling as excited as anyone has a right to feel. I pulled up big as life in front of Bobbie's house. She came out and when I told her, we jumped and screamed, got in the car, and headed to Gloria's house to show her.

Now, with my new car, I could drive Kenneth home to Saranac Lake some Friday nights. On Sunday night, he would tell me how much he missed me over the weekend. I believed him until I found out he had a girlfriend in Saranac Lake. I refused to see him until he stopped seeing her. Just before I turned eighteen, Kenneth broke up with his girlfriend, but I was getting ready to move on to a new school, new boys, and new bars.

CHAPTER 23

COLLEGE AND CAR CRASH

On my eighteenth birthday, my mother threw me a birthday party. For the first time, I could drink legally in the bar. Little did my mother know, I had been drinking illegally in our bar for years. I never had a problem sneaking out, because my mother worked so hard, when she went to sleep nothing woke her.

At this time, I was preparing to go to Adirondack Community College in Hudson Falls, located approximately one hour from Long Lake. I was excited about this new venture, but it presented two problems. First, I had to come home every weekend and tend bar to help pay for college. Second, I had to stay with an old woman, Mrs. Martin, instead of in an apartment with roommates.

Immediately, I began lying to Mrs. Martin. I told her I drove down on Monday mornings and went right to class. Actually, I drove down on Sunday nights, and stayed at my girlfriends' apartment, so I could go out and party.

I was angry when Mom told me I had to stay with Mrs. Martin. When I blurted out that Venita didn't stay with a chaperone when she went to beauty school, Mom responded with, "But, Gail, she was much more mature at eighteen than you are."

"So, you don't trust me," I replied.

"No, Gail, I don't right now, but maybe next year." I could hardly argue with her. She had caught me sneaking out several times and drunk a couple of times. Moreover, I didn't want to ruin my Sunday night lie, so I dropped it. However, I did figure another angle. I told my parents that I had to take Algebra on Saturday morning because it was the only class left open to freshman. That way, I could party Friday night and come home Saturday. It worked the first week. During the second week, disbelieving Kenneth called the school and discovered there were no Saturday classes. He quickly told my parents and that night Dad called and said, "So Gail, what class was it that you had on Saturday morning?"

"Uh, Algebra," I lied.

"Good try, honey, but we know there are no Saturday classes. Kenneth called the school. You will come home this Friday to tend bar, right?"

"Right, Dad," I stammered, embarrassed that he found out and mad as a cornered raccoon at Kenneth. As soon as I saw him Friday night, I broke up with him. He tried to say he didn't do it, and when I threatened to tell Dad that Ken called him a liar, he came clean. I couldn't believe how well it all worked out for me. I had a great excuse to dump him, so I could date the college boys, and my Sunday party night remained intact.

Now, every Friday night I picked up Gloria, who was attending school in Albany, and we shot up the Northway to Long Lake; however, on one of those Friday nights we didn't make it home. That night, in Glens Falls, the weather was calm as I prepared to leave for home. I did not know about a terrible ice storm ravaging the high peaks region. In Long Lake, Mom was busy cooking. Around 4:00 PM, she looked out the window and saw snow coming down. Customers were coming in buzzing about the ice storm brewing outside. Mom made a mental note to call me when Avis got there to relieve her; however, the restaurant became extremely busy, because of stranded motorists, and she forgot to call.

My friend, Robin, was coming home with me that weekend, and I had picked up Gloria around 6:00 PM. When we reached Minerva, we ran into snow, and when we reached the top of Minerva hill, it became freezing rain. The road was glare ice. I began to position the wheels on the car so the right two were in the snow on the side of the road and the left two were on the road. Growing up in the Adirondacks, I had learned to position tires in the snow if the road was icy. The tires on the side would then have traction on the snow. All four tires were still on the road as the car began to slide a little toward the side. Since I was down to about 10 miles an hour, I knew this was fine as long as I didn't hit the brakes until I heard the tires on the snow. Besides, there was a snow bank a foot from side of the road, so we would have a soft landing even if we slid too much. I heard the front tire on the snow and suddenly saw a hand reach over and grab my steering wheel yanking it hard to the left. I was stunned. I looked over at Robin who was screaming, "We're going to crash!" "We're going to crash!" Her fist was tightly wrapped around my steering wheel.

I yelled, "We are now! Get your hands off the wheel!" I pulled her hand off the wheel, but now we were spinning like a top down the middle of this mountain road picking up speed as the car circled faster and faster on the ice. We were on solid ice, so there was nothing I could do. We spun about 25 feet down the road and ended up on the opposite side with the front end and right side of the car over the guardrails. I sat in stunned silence, and then looked over to my right. Gloria was in the passenger's seat and her side of the car was up in the air. "Gloria, are you okay?"

"Yes, I'm fine, scared as Hell, but not hurt."

"Better slide down toward me and we will all get out my door." Luckily, I was able to open my door and the three of us slid out onto the road where we all promptly fell again on the ice. "That hurt. How could we drive on this stuff when we can't even walk?" Robin lamented as she picked herself up off the road.

"That is why I was trying to get to the side of the road, Robin; I can't believe you did that to us. I can't believe you grabbed my steering wheel." We began walking toward Newcomb staying well over to the side of the road. Gloria and I knew that we might be in for a long cold walk. We were in the middle of nowhere on a sparsely traveled road. I thought, who is going to be on this road on a night like this? Robin did not know how far we were from another town. She was from the south and not accustomed to the severe weather of the Adirondacks. She also did not have a driver's license, and I was so mad at her as we trudged up the Newcomb road, wind and snow slapping us in the face, that I could not even look at her. She kept whining, "I'm sorry. I'm so sorry, Gail. I guess I just panicked."

"Forget it Robin, just walk," I snapped back.

Gloria was equally furious at Robin and was saying things like, "How could you do such a dumb thing, especially since you don't even have a license?"

Then we got the bright idea of singing, "Hey, lets sing; it's over, and it doesn't matter how it happened. Somebody will come along," I said. I began to sing one of the popular songs and then all three of us were singing at the top of our lungs, laughing, and joking about how we would remember this for the rest of our lives.

Finally, Gloria yelled, "Hey, look, lights!" We all searched down the road, and sure enough, there was a lone car ambling up the road barely visible in the midst of the heavy snowfall. The three of us stood in the middle of the road, arms flailing. The driver stopped. He was on his way to Minerva, but picked us up and took us to Newcomb, which was 10 miles in the opposite direction. We had walked five miles in the blizzard. I called home and talked to Dad, so fearful to tell him what happened.

I said, "Dad, we have had an accident. I am so sorry."

"Is anyone hurt?" he asked..

"No, we are okay, but the car…"

"Don't worry about the car. As long as you girls are all right, that is all that matters. I'll send someone to pick you up." I breathed a sigh of relief and within thirty minutes, Steve

100

Jennings pulled up and we all piled into his wonderful warm vehicle. Later I found out that the bumper and tire of my car needed replacement, which totaled $600.00 worth of damage. I never invited Robin home again.

CHAPTER 24

STORMY WEATHER AHEAD

On another treacherous winter night about three weeks later, I was in my college friends' apartment with my latest friend, Danny. We were all drinking and discussing the howling blizzard of a storm outside when all of sudden, we heard a knock on the door. Someone said, "Who, in their right mind, would be out in this storm? Willa opened the door and there, standing in the doorway, covered in snow was Kenneth.

"Is Gail here?" he asked.

I could not believe my ears. I got up and met him at the door. "What are you doing here?" I stammered, glancing back at Danny feeling awkward and afraid.

"I came to see you. What do you think? I haven't heard from you in two weeks."

"I know, because I broke up with you." He looked past me, saw Danny standing behind me, and immediately figured out the situation. In an instant, he blew past me, grabbed Danny by the shirt, and shouted, "What in the hell is going on here?" His face popped red and his body shook. He picked up Danny like a doll and threw him against the wall. Kenneth was thin, but he lifted propane gas tanks all day, and that, plus his rage made him a dangerous man.

"Ken, I am not his girlfriend and even if I was, you have no right to break in here!" "Get to hell out of my house!" I shouted. I was mortified. I had never seen a man get this mad except my father when he was drunk. Kenneth was not drunk.

With that, he let go of Danny, but planted himself in a nearby chair.

"Hey, I don't want any trouble," Danny said grabbing his coat off the chair, his brown eyes searing through me like a sword. He and his friend, Tom, took their six packs of beer and slammed out the door. Well, I guess I won't be seeing him again, I thought. After yelling at Ken for ten minutes, I introduced him to my friends and we all sat down and had a drink.

Later, in the kitchen, I told him that I thought he was crazy for coming here on such a night, but underneath I was enamored that he would go to such links to capture me.

"I love you," he replied. "I had to see you." "Gail, I would do anything for you, just please say you'll stay with me." After much more talking, we made up. He stayed and pleaded with me as he always did to let him go all the way. We were in the middle bedroom on the bed kissing, breathing heavily in the throes of intimacy. He was trying; I was saying no. Then, I thought, I am the only eighteen-year-old girl in my group who has never had sex. I did love this man so why not with him. I told him I was worried about getting pregnant. He said, "Come on, Gail, a woman can't get pregnant the first time."

"Really, are you sure?" He was 23 and had been around. I was barely 18 and knew nothing about the world outside my little mountain town.

"Yes, I'm sure," said the spider to the fly and that night in Glens Falls, I became a woman. I hated sex. It hurt, was disgusting, and I vowed I would never do it again.

Later, I told my married friend, Rob, what we did. He asked if we used a condom. I responded naively that I could not get pregnant the first time. He laughed. "Is that what he told you?"

"Yes."

"Not true, Gail." He shook his head no, and within three months, I was puking every morning before classes, and passing out in classrooms and getting fat.

I told Kenneth, and he said I might be pregnant. He said I needed to see Doc Hosley to find out. Doc was the Long Lake doctor, and I was too embarrassed to see him, so Kenneth took

104

me to Dr. Rita in Tupper Lake. She confirmed that I was pregnant. I was terrified and Kenneth was happy. He said, "We have to get married." Two months ago, I was breaking up with this man, and now I was contemplating marrying him. I was confused, scared, and did not know what to do, so I did what he said. He said to get married, so a week later a justice of the peace in Queensbury, NY married us. That night we drove to Venita's house, who was married by now, and that was our honeymoon. We had no money and no place to live. I called Mom from Venita's and said, "Mom, I'm married." After she almost passed out, I told her some rubbish about how I loved him, he loved me, and we had been talking about getting married since September. Half of that statement was true because we had discussed it, and I had rejected it; however, in my world, anything that was half-true became true if I wished it so. The next news came after I came home. "Mom, I'm pregnant." College had lasted one semester.

CHAPTER 25

MISCARRIAGE AND MISGIVINGS

Kenneth and I moved in with my parents, and I cleaned and waitressed for our rent. My brother, Mike, was furious at me because I had not told him I was getting married. I did say to him the evening before, after dad had bellowed out something as he was walking through the dining room that I would never have to hear that again. Mike asked why and I said, "Because I'm getting out of here. He did not believe me because I said that many times before. I reverted to my silent self when the pregnancy shock hit me, so I could not tell him, even though we were so close.

One day about two months after our marriage, I began to feel very sick. I had swollen up terribly in the last five months and kept passing out, but I hid it from my mother. I did not want to go to Doc Hosley because I was ashamed, so I went once again to Dr. Rita in Tupper Lake. She gave me vitamins and told me to come back in a month. I did not.

During the pregnancy, I had experienced some nausea in the morning. Now, I was nauseated all the time. This escalated into cramping in my stomach. It was winter in the Adirondacks, and many people had a stomach flu at the time. I thought, oh great, I have the flu. I went to Doc Hosley and told him my symptoms and he confirmed my prognosis, that I had the flu. He did not know I was pregnant. He prescribed antibiotics and sent me home. The next few days, I began to feel better. I was holding food down and the cramping had almost diminished. However, on the third day at about 10:00 AM, I was in the living room when a cramp hit me so hard; I doubled over in pain. I could not move or speak. Then, I felt something running down my legs. I screamed for Mom who was in the kitchen. She ran in and managed to get me into the bathroom. "Mom, what's happening to me?" I cried.

"Gail, I think you are having a miscarriage. You have to go to the hospital."

"Okay, I cried, get Kenneth."

"He's way up in Brandeth Lake." I knew there was no way to contact him and by now, I knew that what was flowing out of me was blood. "Gail, don't move. I'll be right back. You will be okay. I'll get Dad."

"No, not Dad," I whimpered, but she was gone. Soon, I heard her hurried footsteps coming back. She gave me pads to absorb the blood and walked me out to the kitchen door where Dad was waiting. They helped me into the big Chrysler and Dad drove me to Tupper Lake Hospital where I lost my first child, a little girl. On the way, I dug my fingers into the upholstery so hard that it left an imprint in the seat. My father said, "Well, now you can leave him and go back to college." I looked at him as if he had two heads. I loved my husband and had no intention of leaving him.

My father was a formidable presence at the hospital, demanding that someone look after his daughter now. I was in so much pain, I was happy he made a scene. They came with a wheelchair, rushed me into a room, and put me in bed. I was shamed and humiliated in that bed and the pains were excruciating, but I knew I deserved them. It was a Catholic hospital and the head nun had taught me Catechism. She knew my mother and her family. She was very cold to me and once again, I knew I was doomed to a fiery future. Doc Hosley came and asked, "Why, Gail, why didn't you tell me?"

"I was too embarrassed," I whispered, covering my face with my hands. He told me I was losing the baby and they would be doing a procedure in a few minutes. He was kind and gentle and I was grateful for him. Kenneth arrived about an hour later, and we held each other and cried over the loss of our first-born child.

I came down with Tonsillitis in the hospital and by the time Kenneth took me home, I had a temperature of 103. I lay in bed for several days and then Kenneth told me we needed to move to Saranac Lake. He had a better job there that would be easier on his back. Against my parents' wishes, we left in the night in the snow with me so feverish and sick I thought I would die. Kenneth drove me straight to the Saranac Lake hospital where the doctor told us it was the worst case of Tonsillitis he ever saw and that I needed to be hospitalized. We did not have insurance, and I refused to go back in the hospital because that is where I got so sick in the first place. After Kenneth pleaded our case, the doctor gave us some powerful medicine, and Kenneth took me to his mother's apartment on Main Street in Saranac Lake. She took care of me as I moved in and out of delirium, at some point, asking Kenneth to kill me to take the pain away. He didn't. I survived and the first day I was well enough to go out, Irene, his mother, took me to the store and bought me a dress for Easter. She was very kind to me, and I was grateful to her.

CHAPTER 26

INSIDE THE RED STAINED GLASS, WINDOWS IN FRONT OF THE CROSS OF JESUS STOOD TWO SOULS BETROTHING THEMSELVES TO THE FLAMES OF MARRIAGE.

Kenneth and I remarried in the Catholic Church with our families attending; hence, I married him twice not knowing either time anything about whom I married.

The first time I realized that something was quite wrong with the man I married was one week after we returned home from our first vows. One morning, I was getting ready to go work. He was brushing his hair.

"Kenneth, I am going to Tupper shopping with Bobbie after work," I said as I finished combing my hair before rushing out.

"No, you aren't," he said.

"What?" I thought I misunderstood him, so I repeated, "Bobbie and I are going to Tupper Lake."

He turned around. His face was red, eyes glaring, "I said, No!"

My mouth dropped. Anger poured through me like hot wax. "What do you mean, No, don't tell me what to do."

"I'm your husband, and I will tell you what to do. You whores are not going anywhere together."

I could not believe what I was hearing. I yelled something back about him being a whore and the next thing I knew, the brush sailed past my head missing me by a fraction of an inch. I grabbed the doorknob. "You're crazy," I shouted as I ran out the door almost crashing into Mom. I bolted across the road to my little bridge behind the red house, and I cried, realizing for the first time that Kenneth could be violent whether he was drunk or sober. I learned that he could be romantic, that he was always sorry when he hit me, that he was worse when he drank, and that in a fight he could trump me every time. I took to hiding in closets and under the bed when he came home drunk. Many times this worked, and soon I began to love the closets and tight spaces under the bed. I could spend hours there. I could spend hours locked in the bathroom. By this time, I had a job putting rawhide on books for sale in gift stores. The building was freezing with perpetual water on the floor and I was sick regularly, so they fired me.

I was relegated to pay the bills because he simply would not pay them. I had to hide money for the rent because he spent it or gambled it on pool games. I was still a teenager, rocketed out of school into a small apartment in Saranac Lake with a man much like my father except he did not need alcohol to become a monster. One morning, I got up to get the money to pay the rent. Once again, it was gone. "Kenneth, where is the money for the rent?"

"I don't know. Where did you put it?" He was always in a hurry. He was buttoning up his white shirt to go to work at the Grand Union where he finally got another job after being fired from the last two for his temper. "God damn it, Gail, you didn't iron this shirt right! I am not wearing this thing. What to hell is wrong with you? Don't you know how to do anything? You are the stupidest bitch I ever met!" On and on he went in this vein until he pulled the shirt off, buttons going everywhere. It was a brand new shirt. I saw there was a tiny crease in the back of the collar.

I grabbed the shirt and shouted, "You don't want this shirt?"

"No, I'm not wearing that thing!"

"Good, then I won't have to iron it!" With that, I opened the kitchen window and threw it out. We lived on the second

112

floor of a store on Lake Flower Ave. The shirt billowed and floated smack into the front yard of the neighbor's house. It was at this point that I knew I was done with the secrets--secrets of my father, and secrets of my husband.

"Jesus, he shouted, now go out and get that and tell them it was accident!"

"No, you tell them. It's your shirt, not mine!" He slapped me. I did not care, and I did not go get it; he could have beaten me raw, kicked me, or threatened me because something snapped and for once, I refused to do what he said.

Our relationship was tumultuous to say the least, but we had our joyful moments, too. I loved to walk in the snow, and he would walk with me. We window shopped at the Saranac Lake stores in the evenings, holding hands, kissing, and talking about our dreams. We became involved in bobsledding. He was the brakeman on a local team, and I was one of the wives who kept score. We went to Catholic mass together and danced our hearts out to songs like, "Pretty Woman." We won a dance contest, played baseball, and went to car races and hockey games. I loved watching him bobsled and play baseball, and for a time the romance and excitement of being with him overcame the darkness of his rage.

CHAPTER 27

RICKY

Ricky was born on December 28, 1965 on a bright, sunshiny morning. He was a small baby with a head as round as a baseball. I fell in love with him immediately, and I vowed that my baby would not grow up in a violent home. I vowed to be the best mother in the world and to protect this beautiful blue-eyed baby boy.

The day I came home from the hospital was December 31. I was excited and scared at the same time. We lived in a tiny bungalow on Lake Flower Avenue. I wanted my baby all to myself, but barbs of fear pricked at me. What if he goes to sleep and I don't hear him wake up? What if he cries and I don't know what he wants? What if I am too stupid to care for a baby? By now, I was convinced I was either mentally challenged or slow. Kenneth repeatedly told me I was dumb, and in high school, when I told the principal I wanted to be a PE teacher, he told me that I was not smart enough. He suggested I go for homemaking because I had high grades in that class. The homemaking tests were so easy for me; I scored one hundred percent on every test even though I hated cooking and sewing. Ironically, the only person who thought I was intelligent was Dad, whose favorite drunk word for me was," Stupid." Sober, he said things like, "That girl is college material; I tell you she is college material." This contradiction was another oxymoron for me to roll around in my brain.

The evening I came home with baby Ricky, I learned that Daddy still planned to go out for New Years Eve. "But, Kenneth, I cried, this is your son, just home for the first night."

"And he'll be home every other night until he is grown, so I will see him everyday." This party has been planned for weeks."

"But, I'm scared to be alone with him. I've never taken care of a new baby before." I had taken turns with Venita each night giving my sister, Sheryl, her nighttime bottles, but that was a long time ago and Mom was asleep in the bedroom. Here, I would be alone with the baby. "Please stay home just this one time," I pleaded. His answer was that I knew where he would be if I needed him. Of course, we didn't have a telephone, so I did not see how it benefited me to know where he was that night; however, I could see by the look on his face that it was shut up time, so I shut up. I shut up for my baby, I shut up for my sanity, and I shut up because the fear of this man trumped the fear of caring for my new baby.

That very night, I learned that this little infant and I were a team to be reckoned with. Ken came into the bedroom around 8:00 PM all dressed up in his new starched white shirt, tie, and new suit coat. I was changing Ricky so his diaper was off. Ken bent over, gave Ricky a kiss just as Ricky let loose and peed all over daddy's new shirt and tie. He was furious. I was trying so hard not to laugh, but I did. He looked at me and said, "So you think this is funny?"

"Yes, I said, he's just a baby, Ken."

Kenneth looked down at Ricky and then, he too, began to laugh. Secretly, I thought, Dad got what he deserved.

I rocked Ricky until after midnight that first night. It was 1966, and we saw the New Year in together. Reluctantly, I put him in his crib and woke up at 4:30 AM terrified that he was dead. I crept in and looked at him, and I could see that he was not breathing. Oh my God, he's dead, I thought. Fear filled every fiber of my body. I could not breathe. I thought I would pass out. Then I felt his chest and discovered that he was breathing. I sat in the chair next to his bed the rest of the night waiting for him to

116

wake up. He didn't wake up until 5:30 AM. His father was still not home.

Ricky was a precocious child from the start. When he was about six months old, he was riding in the back seat of our Studebaker. It was a 1966, before seat belts and car seats. Ricky found the door handle and pushed it down hard enough to open the door. Kenneth was driving very slowly in front of the Saranac Lake Park. Just as Ricky tumbled out the door, Kenneth glanced in the rearview mirror, and immediately slammed on the brakes. I jumped out of the car, ran to the back and there was Ricky lying directly in front of the back tire, the tire being only an inch from his stomach. He was not even crying. I grabbed him, hugged him, and almost fainted, having to sit down on the bench. Kenneth and I both looked him over from head to toe. He was fine. We shook and cried for about ten minutes before we could get back in the car and drive home. As soon as we got home, Ken was out the door with a wrench. We no longer had back door handles in that car.

By the time Ricky was ten months old, we knew he loved animals. We took him to the petting park where he squealed with delight when he touched the deer and sheep. One day in mid September, we took him to The Thousand Animals, an animal park on the outskirts of Lake Placid. He raced around that place, awed by all the animals. He had a wonderful time, ate lunch and dinner, and went right to sleep when I put him in his crib for the night. Around 2:00 AM, I heard a noise emanating from his room. I jumped up and hurried into his room. Flicking on the light, I immediately saw that his cheeks were fiery red, and heard him moaning. I picked him up. "Ricky, Ricky, it's Mommy, look at Mommy." He looked up at me and his beautiful blue eyes rolled back in his head. All I saw was white. "Kenneth, I screamed, Kenneth!" He came running into the room.

"What, what's going on?"

"It's the baby, get me a baby aspirin."

He ran into the bathroom and came back with the baby aspirin. When I put the aspirin on Ricky's tongue, it stuck there. "Oh my God, we've got to get him to the hospital." "Call the ambulance."

"No, wrap him in the blanket. We'll get him there faster ourselves," he gasped as he ran to put his pants on. I threw on pants, tucked my nightgown inside, grabbed a blanket, and wrapped Ricky up in it. Thank God, the hospital was only three blocks away. Kenneth drove like a lunatic, right up to the emergency room. I ran in with the baby, met a nurse, she looked at Ricky, grabbed him from my arms, and rushed down the hospital corridor with him.

By now, I was crying and Ken and I were wrapped in each other's arms in silent prayer. Soon the nurse came back and told us that they had immersed him in ice to get his temperature down. He had a temperature of 107. Later on, the doctor came and told us that he had pneumonia. We couldn't believe it. How could our baby have such happy day, be perfectly fine and four hours later have pneumonia? He told us that a baby's temperature could spike for no reason. Ricky's did, but he assured us our baby would recover after a few days in the hospital. During those days, you could not stay in this hospital with your loved one. I could not imagine going home without my baby, but we did.

Keeping this little tiger in a crib was not an easy task. The second day he was there, the nurses were talking at their station when they heard a tiny voice say, "Hi." They looked up and here was this little tyke strolling down the hall, big as life. The nurses could not figure out how he got out of those tall iron barred cribs, but he did. They put him back, and he was out again within minutes, so they had to put a cage over his bed. It broke our hearts to see him in a cage. I would hold him, and when I had to leave, he would scream. The only thing he wanted was to be with mommy, and all I wanted was to be with him. The doctor barred me from coming for two days, so he could settle down and they could get his temperature down. It spiked when I had to leave him. I could not stay with him, so Kenneth, Grandma Irene and Grandpa Charles went for the next two days.. It was a nightmare and I longed for my baby. I was elated when Doc told us on the fifth day that we could take him home.

Ricky's first birthday
Author, Ricky, Kenneth

CHAPTER 28

MONTI

We began to try for a second child because we wanted them close in age, and soon I found out I was pregnant. This meant we needed to move out of our little bungalow on the hill. We found an upstairs apartment above a grocery store right down the street and moved in. I met Vicky and Homer Burgoyne, my neighbors. He had a band and played in all the local clubs and she was a stay-at-home Mom with three kids. Vicky and I immediately became friends, our common bonds being children and disappearing husbands.

Monti came a few months after moving to the store apartment. On the morning of March 15, 1967, I began to have contractions. I called Kenneth at the Grand Union where he worked. He came home and took me to the hospital. Three hours later, I was no longer having contractions. The doctor sent me home and Kenneth went back to work. Within 30 minutes, the contractions started again only minutes apart. Kenneth rushed home again; we got in the car and began racing to the hospital. Suddenly, we saw red lights flashing behind us. "I don't believe this, Ken said, the police are behind us."

"What, you've got to be kidding," I said as I turned my head and saw the white car and flashing lights behind us. Soon the state trooper appeared in Kenneth's window.

As soon as the officer approached the window, Ken said, "Please officer, my wife is having a baby." "The contractions are three minutes apart and we're trying to get to the Lake Placid Hospital."

He said, "Oh my, okay, follow me, I'll give you a police escort." Therefore, Monti's arrival was a fireworks affair from the start. We arrived at the hospital red lights spinning, and siren blaring. That police officer did not want to deliver a baby that day. In addition, Dr. Hart had just gone home and could not get back in time. I remember Kenneth running down the hall yelling, "Where is the damn doctor?" He was an animated man anyway, and now he was a screaming psycho. I shouted, "Ken, get back in here with me; I am having this baby now!"

A nurse ran in, checked me, and repeated, "She's right, this baby is coming now." She went to the closet, took out a gown and mask, threw it at Ken and said, "Put this on, we're delivering your baby."

"But, I can't…"

"You have to help me." "I can't lift her by myself." "I'll be right back." She came back with a table and by this time, Ken had the gown on. They lifted me onto the table and whisked me into the delivery room. Monti arrived within fifteen minutes. There was no time for any anesthesia or doctor.

During my pregnancy, I was continually plagued with a premonition about this child. I dreamed he was handicapped with a clubfoot. No matter what the nurse told me, I did not believe her, until I saw him. Of course, the moment I saw him, I was in love with this little baby. He had jet-black hair reaching down to his neck and a tiny scrunched up face He looked just like his Grandpa Jakes. He did not have a clubfoot, but I still harbored a foreboding feeling that something was wrong. His skin was not right. His breathing was not right. The doctor told me it was just mucus, and it would soon clear up. He sent me home with reassurances that my baby was fine.

Within two weeks, I knew he was wrong. I called the doctor again. Again, he told me not to worry, that his breathing problem was just mucus. He repeated this mantra to me during his next checkup even though I told him that Monti was projectile vomiting and not getting fatter like Ricky did.

Finally, after another week went by with no change, I flatly told the doctor that I wanted to see a specialist. He made an appointment for Monti to have tests done at DeGoesbriand Hospital in Burlington, VT. It was a renowned children's hospital. I will never forget the day Kenneth and I drove to the hospital and placed him in a little crib next to a dying baby with water on the brain. The terror that went through me when I saw this precious child was like a cold sharp icicle slowly inching downward through my body. They did not let either of us stay at the hospital, so we had to walk out of that institution at night, leaving our infant son. It was excruciatingly painful. We came to see him every day, riding the ferry over from New York to Burlington. We were devastated when he tested positive for cystic fibrosis. They did a second test and that one came back positive, too.

In the meantime, we tried to give Ricky all the love and nurturing he needed. He was only fourteen months old. Between his Grandpa Charles, Grandma Irene, Kenneth, and I, we were able to manage this, but it took the whole family. This would not be the only time we had to team up and keep vigil over our children.

I called my mother and talked to her. I cried and told her that her grandson had this horrible disease that would cut his life short. She told me to ask them to run the test one more time. I did, and this time, the test came back negative. We were mixed with joy and sorrow because he didn't have Cystic Fibrosis, but now we were back to square one and time was running out. He was not keeping food down, losing weight, and dangerously thin.

Finally, one of the resident hospital students said, "Well, there is one other thing we haven't tried."

"What, what is it?" I was willing to do anything at this point.

"We haven't tested him for allergies."

"Allergies, really, it could be that?"

"I don't think it is, but just to rule it out, we are going to set you up with an allergist. Can you come back tomorrow?"

Kenneth and I looked at each other both nodding yes, not knowing what else to do. The doctor made the appointment. I took my baby in, held him while they scraped his little back with needles, and immediately large welts began popping up everywhere. Monti was allergic to over 60 items, one being the formula I kept trying to feed him so he would not starve to death. I was relieved that it was something we could control and for the first time since before his birth, that impending feeling of doom began to dissipate.

I brought him home and began the daily routine of washing everything in his room, and covering holes in his crib mattress because he was allergic to dust and mattress stuffing. We bought expensive formula for him because he was allergic to all dairy and wheat. Finally, he began to grow, and he grew into the most beautiful brown-eyed stocky little boy anybody ever had.

Monti

Due to his allergies, Monti was sick quite often. One time, he got bronchitis so badly; he could not breathe lying down. The hospital was full and the doctor told us we would have to prop him up on pillows and keep vigil over him all night to make sure he stayed in a seated position while he slept. I was terrified, but we all went over to Charles and Irene's apartment and slept there with each of us taking shifts. I barely slept at all those nights because I was so scared. We did this for three nights until the medicine starting taking effect, and he could breathe freely. I will forever be grateful to those wonderful grandparents who were there when we needed them.

By the time Monti was two years old, he had grown out of most of these allergies; however, that was not the only catastrophe we dealt with in our children's young lives.

One night when Monti was still an infant and Vicky's and my husband were out partying, I woke up smelling smoke. I opened my eyes, jumped out of bed, grabbed the boys, ran through a blanket of smoke next door, and banged on Vicky's door. "Fire, Fire, I screamed, Vicky, get up, we've got to get out of here!"

Finally, she came to the door. "What?"

"Get the kids, Vicky, there is a fire!"

She snapped to attention, "Gail, take the boys, outside. I'll get my kids!" I ran down the stairs, out the door, looked up, and saw flames downstairs under my apartment.

"Vicky, hurry," I screamed! Within seconds, she came bounding down the stairs with her three kids.

Neither of us had a telephone, the store was closed, and the temperature was below freezing.. "I'll run up to the pay phone and call the fire department." "Stay here with the kids," Vicky said as she sped off up the road. The children and I huddled together to keep warm. All of our noses had black soot coming out of them. I feared for Monti's well being because of his breathing problems. Soon sirens echoed in the cold night air, and I saw Vicky running back down the road.

A police car turned in, parked in the parking lot, and we gladly got in the warm car. Fire engines raced up Lake Flower, and surged into the parking lot. We watched the firefighters in their slick black coats smash open the store door with an ax and rush inside. Ricky was now wide-awake squealing with delight at sight of the big red truck. A few minutes later, the fire chief opened the door and told me that it was an electrical fire in the store below my apartment. He said, "You will have to stay somewhere tonight."

I hadn't thought of that. "Uh, my husband is out in one of the bars, but I don't know which one." Hot anger began to sear through my veins as it dawned on me that we could have died if I wasn't such a light sleeper, and because of his drinking, we had no money for a damn telephone. I began to cry, "I don't know what to do." Then I thought of Ken's father." Would you call his father, Charles, please?"

"We will do that, and we will find Kenneth too." I told him what bars I thought he might be in and they radioed into the police dispatchers to find our husbands. They already knew where to find Ken because he grew up there and everybody in the little town knew him.. Amazingly, Charles, Kenneth, and Vicky's husband all pulled into the parking lot at the same time.

It was 2:00 AM, two hours after I first woke up, and now I began to hear, "Oh my God, Gail," I am so sorry I wasn't here." Kenneth cried, and I held him assuring him that we were all okay. Then, I saw his father's face above him wracked with pain and anguish at the inadequacy and irresponsibility of his son. We stayed with Charles for the next few weeks until the apartment was habitable. The first Friday night we were back, Ken rolled in at 3:00 AM that morning. I learned that I'm sorry meant I'm lying, and I learned that I was the lone protector of my children. On Monday, I stole money from the vault at my job

126

and purchased telephone service. On Friday, when Ken was paid, I stole money from his wallet while he was showering and paid back the stolen money. He noticed it missing much later, and thought it fell out of his wallet, or someone stole it. Since he did not pay the bills, when the telephone showed up, he did not question how I paid for it. I soon became versed in stealing and hiding money for rent, food, and utilities. I stole money from his wallet after he passed out, but each day I became more resentful over the tiring task of working full-time, caring for two toddlers, and constantly figuring out ways to exist in this horrendous one-sided world.

Top L, cousin, Scot, Ricky, cousin, Dana, Monti

CHAPTER 29

DAVEY

In the fall of 1966, Cohen's plumbing company in Saranac Lake hired me to work in the office, running the cash register, and preparing the paperwork for drivers. Our trucks delivered parts all through the North Country. On May 17, 1967 around 10:00 AM, I began to sense a darkness permeating through my body like a slithering snake. It felt like something bad was going to happen. I was jumpy and scared every time the phone rang. I kept telling my co-worker that I felt very uncomfortable. Around 2:30, the telephone rang and the receptionist answered it. I heard, "Oh my God."

She gave the telephone to my boss. I heard, "Where?" and "Are you sure?" He hung up, put the phone down, and ran his fingers through his dark hair. His face was all pinched. He looked at us and said, "Bucky has hit a child."

Immediately, I felt as if my head would explode, "What? Where, where did it happen?"

"Oh God, I don't remember. Jesus, where was it?"

"Long Lake," I said because I knew.

"Yes, that was it, Long Lake."

I had no explanation how I knew, but I asked, "Was it a little boy?"

"Yes, it was a boy." There were tears in his eyes and my hands began to tremble.

"My God, Gail, you said something bad was going to happen," my coworker uttered. "Is it somebody you know?"

"Yes, it's my nephew, I whispered" Earlier I knew it was either my sister, Sheryl, or Larry's son, Davey. Now, that Bill said it was a boy, I was sure it was Davey. For the next hour, the phones were busy with my boss talking to Bucky, and the police.

Finally, it rang, and it was for me. It was my sister, Venita, telling me what happened. Davey had gone with my sister, Sheryl, across the road from the Lakeside to pick blueberries. They were waiting to cross back over and Sheryl was holding his hand. Before she left to go downtown, his mother had told him not to cross the street. He did not tell his Aunt Sheryl this. While Sheryl and he were waiting for a car to pass in front of them, Davey saw his mother's truck coming back. As soon as the car went by, he pulled out of Sheryl's grasp to run quickly across the road before his mother saw him. He ran right into the fully loaded plumbing truck that was behind the car. He never saw the truck and Bucky could not stop in time even though he slammed on the brakes.

My father ran out and held his head, but little Davey never regained consciousness. He was pronounced dead at Tupper Lake hospital. The funeral was horrific. He was a beautiful blonde haired, blue eyed bouncing boy just beginning life, ironically, struck down by the delivery truck I had watched pull out of the parking lot 50 miles away that morning. The whole town came as they always did when it was one of their own. They were wonderful and did all they could to comfort Larry and Betty, but tragedies cut deep and this one still remains a wound in the hearts of our family, especially with, Sheryl, who was torn with guilt. Larry and Betty were devastated forever bearing the heartache of a mother and father witnessing the death of their child.

CHAPTER 30

END OF A MARRIAGE

Monti was two months old when we lost Davey, and throughout that fall and winter, I transformed from wanting my husband to be home with me to hoping he would stay out all night. I never knew what was going to happen when he came home, and I was constantly trying to keep his yelling down so the boys did not wake up. I had learned that love can be worn away one word at a time, and now I was only there so my children had a father.

Sometimes when he hit me, I ran to the church rectory to Father Tucker, for help. Several times, Father came to the house and talked to Kenneth. Several times, I slept in the rectory with black eyes, and several times, I called the police, but these police officers had grown up with Kenneth, so they would not help me.

If we went out and I happened to turn around to see who was coming through the door, he accused me of flirting. If I spoke to any male while we were out, he accused me of having an affair. My solution to this jealousy was to stay home as much as possible. I only went out with him if he insisted.

In addition to his insanity, my mother-in-law, who told me many times that I was the best thing that ever happened to her son, warned me that should I leave, she would help him take my children away from me. I was 21 years old with two toddlers, no education, living in my husband's town. I felt alone, helpless, and confused. Many times, I sat in the bathroom contemplating suicide, knowing in the end, I could not because of my boys. I promised my children that they would never go through what I did and yet, here I was, completely powerless over this violent man. I had also bought into the phrase "You made your bed, now lie in it." I knew it was my fault, and I had to try to do better. Then everything would be all right.

On the other hand, Ken and his mother and father were wonderful to the children. He loved his boys. He called Ricky "Daddy's Man" and never laid a hand on him. Ricky adored his grandfather. He walked to Grandpa Jake's at nine months old because he wanted his hat. Grandpa brought them candy and took us all fishing. He was a kind, generous man and Irene was a loving grandmother. I wanted my children to stay in their lives. I wanted my boys to have a father, and so I stayed.

Early one morning in March of 1968, Kenneth got mad at me, threw me down on the bed, and starting choking me as he had done many times before. I gasped for air and thought, "*this time he is going to kill me.*" I could not breathe. Within the recesses of my mind, I thought I heard a tiny cry. Instantly, I felt Kenneth's grip loosening on my throat. I opened my eyes, and, to my dismay, there stood my little tow headed Ricky grabbing Kenneth's wrist with both of his hands crying, "No, Daddy, No." Kenneth got up, left the room, and Ricky ran to me. I held him tight, cried, and vowed that this little boy would never witness such violence again. That was the finale of my marriage.

My lessons in life taught me that no bees sting if you always watch out for yourself and your children, and that is what I did. Within one year of my new baby's birth, we were out of that violent house. I picked up my children and all their toys and clothes that would fit in couple of boxes, and brought them to a knotty pine cottage in Long Lake under the protection of two brothers, a father, and a bolted down door. My amazing brother, Larry, came to Saranac Lake and moved me out to the safety of my little hometown in the woods.

One night shortly after moving to Long Lake, I heard the front screen door creak. It was about midnight. I grabbed the baseball bat beside my bed and slowly crept up against the living room wall and looked out at the front door. Then I heard

Kenneth yell, "You F...bitch, open this door right now!" I ran to the telephone and called my brother, Mike, who was on leave from Marine Corp boot camp before going to Vietnam. I could hear Kenneth rattling the door handle and yelling that if I did not let him in, he would bust the window. I came out, stood in front of the door, and told him to leave. "I want to see my kids," he hissed.

"You can see them when you're sober!" "You are not seeing them tonight!" "They are sleeping." I said these things knowing that when he was drunk nothing mattered but what he wanted. I knew he would break the window if I did not let him in. I said, "Just a minute, Kenneth, and I will let you in." I went back to the bedroom, loaded my 22, checked on my sleeping boys, shut the door, and walked into the kitchen. Just as I rounded the corner, I heard my older brother, Larry's voice, "What's going on out here?"

Then I heard my father, "Ken, what to hell are you doing here?"

I saw Kenneth turn around and look. I stood in front of the door and saw three large figures coming toward him. I heard my father say, "Come on, lad, you better go on home, or get a room for the night." He immediately left, and made his visits ahead in the daytime. He tried one more night break in about six months later, but my brother ran him off again.

After that, I did not see him for two years. He escaped to Florida after the divorce. There was no financial help, and I did not want any. I would take care of my children and always protect them. It felt like the warden had just unlocked me from prison. I played games with the boys. We watched TV together and slid down the hill on sleds and flying saucers. I made birthday cakes that looked like trains, baseballs, and rockets, and on Thursday nights, we ate pizza and danced around the living room with my favorite singer, Tom Jones. We had play dates with their cousins, Dana and Scot Gagnier and their best friend,

Charlie Bean. We were a team and no bees stung us as long as we were together.

CHAPTER 31

BLUE SKIES, WHITE SNOW, LITTLE ONES TUCKED SOUNDLY IN THEIR BEDS, FOOD IN THEIR BELLIES AND A SIX-PACK FOR MOM.

We lived in the little cabin behind Stanley and Rita Arsenault's large white house on the Newcomb Road. It was a wonderful knotty pine bungalow and in the winter, the kids and I lived on a $33.00 week unemployment check, but I was happy. I spent mornings doing laundry or playing with the kids or drinking coffee with my friends, Joanie and Pat. Pat's little redheaded boy, Charlie, became fast friends with Ricky who was now three years old and faster than a freight train running all day and night. He was sensitive, sweet, and cute with his light blond hair, big blue eyes and turned up nose. He was exceptionally curious, which got him into trouble more than once. The Arsenaults' had two children, Peggy and Bruce, who babysat for me. Bruce became like a second son to me, staying overnight quite frequently. He was wonderful to the boys and they loved him.

I began to worry about the ramifications if something should happen to me when I was alone with the boys. I decided to teach Ricky how to dial 911 and give out our address just in case anything ever happened to Mommy. He learned quickly, and the next day I went off to work at the Lakeside Lodge.

At about 11:00 AM, a police car pulled up in front of the restaurant and an officer came in.

"Good morning, Glen," I said grabbing the menu to give him as he walked in the door.

"Gail, hasn't anyone called you?" he asked.

"Called me, for what?" "Glen, has something happened to the kids?" I began to panic and my voice ended on a high pitch.

"Whoa, hold on, the boys are ok but something did happen. Apparently, when your sitter went outside to hang up clothes this morning, your oldest boy ran inside, called the police, and told the dispatcher that his Mommy was on the floor, and he could not wake her up, and Bruce was dead. Within minutes, all the police cars in the area converged on your house. Your babysitter, Peggy, was just walking into the house, and knew nothing about it until she saw all the cars coming in the driveway."

I was mortified. On top of the whole police department rushing to my house, my sister heard it on the scanner because her husband was a state trooper, so she rushed up to the house. When she pulled in the driveway, there was Ricky climbing his little tree and Peggy staring in disbelief at the police cars rolling in the driveway. This little boy proved to be a fast learner, always curious to discover how things worked. Another time, he started a campfire on the side of the hill because he saw them do it on TV in boy scouts.

His brother, Monti, was just the opposite. He tried to walk at ten months, fell, and refused to venture out again until fifteen months old. People would look at me questioningly as if to say, is there something wrong with that kid. Why can't he walk? He just didn't think he needed to. It was not worth the risk of falling to him. He also rode a skateboard until he was 20 years old instead of getting his drivers license. He rode it to work and everywhere he went. When he was born, my mother said, "Now, I have my little Frenchman," because he had black hair and brown eyes. All of her five children had blue eyes and most of us had light brown, brown, blonde, or red hair. Monti was a beautiful baby and everybody thought he was a girl. He had thick black hair and large brown eyes with long lashes. After being sick the first few months of his life, he began to fill out and became a stocky boy with his father's sense of humor. He was the opposite of his brother in that he took his time to do things, clung to me, and did whatever he was told. He idolized his brother and followed him everywhere doing whatever Ricky did. They were only fourteen months apart and soon became inseparable. However, for me it was like having twins—they were both in diapers at the same time, and I have memories of washing and hanging lines and lines of diapers in the wee hours after working all day. Being a single Mom with two little boys under four did not allow for many hours of sleep.

There were wonderful times such as sliding in the snow, making snowmen, going to Glens Falls to see Disney on Parade, Frontier Town, and the Enchanted Forest. . There were birthday parties, going to grandpas for sugar on snow and playing downstairs with Charlie and their cousins on their big wheels.

My father, my grandfather, and great grandfather on down the line had sugar shanties and made maple syrup. When we were kids, we rode on the back of the truck, gathering sap from Maple trees. The sugarhouse was an old house down the hill from the restaurant. When you opened the door during cooking time, the hot steam and sweet maple aroma blasted you in the face. It always gave me a nostalgic feeling, as if I was back in the 1800s walking into a log shanty, after stepping down from a horse drawn sleigh. Every year, Dad made maple candies and sugar on snow. He invited all the children, and we all sat outside the sugar shanty eating the wonderful taffy-like strips pulled from the pans of snow. He poured the hot liquid on the snow, which immediately turned into the taffy texture. I was happy my children could experience this little bit of American and family culture. I do not know if my father tried to make amends through his grandchildren, or if age mellowed him, but he was kind and caring to them, and they loved him.

During this time, I would occasionally drink a six-pack of beer. The four of us, Ricky, Monti, the dog, and me, would sit on the couch and watch TV while I drank my beer, and they ate their ice cream or whatever bedtime snack they had. Their father had not contacted me since moving to Florida and I was happy. Ricky missed his father, but Monti was too young to remember him. My heart broke when Ricky would get mad and say, "I want my daddy," but I knew that leaving their father was the best thing I could have done for him, and so in the wee hours of the night when the children were safe in their beds, I cried. I cried for the father they would never have, I cried for fear of not having enough money to feed my them, and I cried for that little girl that ran among the rose bushes so fearless, free, and full of love. I cried until I met a man named Mike Tracy.

CHAPTER 32

WHY IS IT THAT AFTER
TWELVE YEARS OF SEEING YOUR SMILE
IN SHATTERED DREAMS,
I STAND RIVETED TO THE BATHROOM FLOOR
HEART FLUTTERING LIKE A SCHOOLGIRL
AT THE SOUND OF
YOUR BOOT STEPS AT MY DOOR?

In November 1968, I met the man who stole my heart and soul. I was tending bar for my father at the Lakeside while he ate his dinner. I reached down to take the cap off a beer for a customer and when I looked up, there he was—blue eyes shining like silver dollars, and dark blond hair jutting out from his cap.

He said, "Hey, beautiful, I know you. Do you remember me?"

I cocked my head, rolled my eyes, and came back with, "I've heard that line at least a thousand times before." I turned, collected the money for the beer, and started washing glasses.

"Hey, wait, I do know you. You're Venita and Larry's sister. You're Gail, right? I'm right, ain't I?"

I looked at him again but I still could not place him. There was something familiar, but I could not remember him.

"I'm Mike, Mike Tracy. Remember, me and Pat used to come in here, and I used to try to get you to serve me, but you knew I wasn't 18 so you wouldn't."

"Mike, is that you?" I asked incredulously. Was this the same toothpick-thin kid I knew when he was sixteen and I was eighteen?

"Yup, it's me, in the flesh."

"Wow, well, where have you been? What ever happened to you?"

"I went into the Navy." "What about you?"

I told him how I had married and had two kids.

"You got married? I never thought you would get married this young, anybody but you, and two kids you say. How old are your kids?"

"I have two boys. They are two and three years old."

"God, you sure are a beautiful woman to have kids" he teased.

"Are you saying, you can't be beautiful and be a mother, too?"

"No, no, that's not what I meant. God, girl you have me all tongue-tied, always did. I had such a crush on you growing up, but you wouldn't give me the time of day. You thought you were too good for a Tracy boy."

"No, I didn't think I was too good. You were too young and too skinny."

"Well, I'm not too young and skinny anymore," he said as he stood up and turned around. This man was definitely not skinny. The Navy had put muscle on him, and I found myself staring at his body, his boyish grin, and his long legs. My heart raced and my whole body began to tingle as I watched him walk across the floor.

"Hey, Gail, how about a drink over here," brought me back to reality as I got a whiskey for Junior at the other end of the bar.

"There you go, Junior." For the last few years, Junior drank whiskey and milk. He was a regular fixture at the bar, drank two drinks, passed out for an hour, woke up, and finished it. He was Bobbie's father and a close friend of my father's.

"Better watch that one, Gail, he ain't no good," Junior, mumbled as he lit his cigarette and began talking to Harold, another regular. I went back to washing glasses and let my mind trickle back to when I first met Mike. Our parents had been friends for years; his Dad and Mom would occasionally come to

140

the bar and bring the kids with them. When he and his brother, Pat, became teenagers, they built a reputation synonymous with the word, "Wild." Wild, in the Adirondacks, meant drinking underage, driving fast and getting into fights.

"Hey, beautiful," Mike leaned over and whispered in my ear, "How long do you have to work tonight?"

"Until my father gets done eating, why?" I shot back.

"I need to leave soon because Danny has to get the car back. Want to ride down to Raquette Lake with us, and I will bring you back?" Come here and meet Danny.

I knew Danny, and he had a reputation, too though milder than Mike's fame.

"Danny, meet Gail. Gail, meet Danny. Ain't she the prettiest woman you ever laid eyes on, Robley?"

Danny laughed. I said, "Hi Danny, nice to meet you." I put out my hand to shake his and Mike took it in his instead.

"Umm, soft hands." "So you're coming with us, right?"

"No, Mike, I am not going anywhere with you."

"Hey, I promise I'll be a good boy. Damn, Gail, you know me. I just want to have a chance to talk to you and catch up on the past, where people are, what you've been doing the past five years." It was true, I knew he would not do anything against my wishes, but I was not worried about him doing anything wrong, I was worried about me. My adrenalin was pumping and I could not believe how happy I felt inside just looking at this man.

I left and said, "I'll think about it, Mike." I went back into the dining room trying to calm myself down. My whole body felt electrified. I had buried any romantic feelings several years ago and thought they were gone. I thought of all the reasons not to go. I had to ask Peggy, my babysitter, if she could stay, I was scared to death, and just as I had convinced myself not to go, I looked up, and there he was standing in front of me with that cockeyed smile.

On that cold November night, I sat in the middle between Robby and Mike and rode to Raquette Lake loving the excitement and the fear I was feeling. I was on the edge, right where I loved to be, talking the whole way about this one and that one, what happened to them, what we had been doing, why we didn't date in high school, and how he was engaged to be married.

"You're engaged!" I repeated incredulously, trying to hide my disappointment.

"Yes, and she's pregnant, so I have to do the right thing. I have to marry her."

Oh my God, I thought, and she's pregnant. After I was able to get a breath, I said, "Do you love her?"

"I don't know," he said. "I guess I thought I did at one time, but I'm not sure now, and I know I don't want to marry her, but I have too."

I felt myself pulling away, immediately going into friend mode. "Does she know you may not love her?"

"I guess not."

"Well, did you tell her you loved her?"

"Well, sure, but not lately."

"God, Mike, well, it looks like you're a married man. When is the wedding?"

"In two weeks."

"Well then, what to hell are you doing flirting with me half the night and dragging me down to Raquette Lake with you?" By this time, we were pulling into the only bar in Raquette Lake. We both got out and stood in the parking lot talking.

He went on, "I just couldn't help it. I saw you sitting in the dining room window when we pulled in and I said to Danny, 'Jesus, who is that woman?' You looked like an angel sitting there in the light. I had no idea it was you. I put my hands on my hips and just shook my head as if I did not know what to do with him. Hey, I'm sorry but I just wanted to talk to you and catch up

142

on all our friends, your parents. Where are Venita and Mike now?"

"Right, I said sarcastically, lets just go have a beer." I started up the wood steps to the bar and once inside; all of Mike's friends came over and introduced themselves to me. I nervously scanned the bar to see if one of them was his fiancée.

It was several beers later on the way home, in the town dump truck, where I learned that Mike had lost his license because of drunk driving, lived in the only motel in Raquette Lake, and took care of sixteen-year-old boy named Luis Burke. Half way home Mike put his arm around me, hugged me until I thought I would melt into him and then bent down and kissed me long and hard. That kiss rocketed me out of reality into another dimension and cemented him in my heart forever.

CHAPTER 33

ON AGAIN OFF AGAIN

Within six months, Mike had broken up with his fiancé and moved in with me. I surrendered to loving him as I had never loved another. I felt guilty about the break up but not guilty enough. I was in love and powerless over whatever he did. We began an emotional roller coaster relationship where he would leave to get a pack of cigarettes and not come back for three days. I would be furious, load up the car with his clothes, and dump them in the parking lot of the motel he lived in when I met him. A day or two later, Mike would call up or come over and beg me to take him back. I would and for another two weeks, bliss ruled.

Mike fell in love with Ricky and Monti; however, at first, they were not thrilled with him. I began to invite Mike to the house to watch television with us. When he came in, Ricky, Monti, and the dog would dart over to the couch and sit next to me forcing him to sit as far away from me as possible. My children had lost their daddy and they were jealous of anyone taking their time away from mommy. After a few weeks of this, Mike began bringing gum for Ricky and Monti, and dog bones for the dog. Bribery worked, and soon the boys and the dog made way for Mike on the couch.

Our relationship was rocky, but not physically violent like my marriage, so I remained somewhat happy, suffering only emotional trauma due to Mike's drinking and promiscuity. By this time, my brother had come home from Vietnam, a hero, honorably completing his stint in the Marine Corp. He and my boyfriend, Mike, became friends and we all partied together. One such party began earlier in Long Lake and ended up with them smashed into a bridge just outside of Inlet. My brother broke both his legs and my boyfriend broke one of his legs.

That winter, my parents took an extended vacation to Florida and left me in charge of the restaurant and both patients. At this time, barhopping was our main sport. Mike Tracy would lift my brother out of his wheelchair, sit him in the back of the car, throw the wheelchair in the back, and off we would go to the Cobblestone or the Wayside in Newcomb. At the Lakeside, my brother would put my son, Ricky, on his lap in the wheelchair, wheel him up to the jukebox, and let Ricky pick songs. He always picked "*Sugar town*" and "*Up Up and Away.*" Mike would also wheel himself behind the bar, grab a bottle of liquor, get drunk and do wheelies in the dancehall. I was a nervous wreck because many wheelies ended up with him upside down on the floor and me taking the whiskey away.

Miraculously, we all survived, and the place was still standing when my parents returned home, but a lot of alcohol was consumed by the management. The only marginally sane one in the bunch was Irma Morrissey, the day bartender, who showed up regularly and didn't drink up all the booze.

During this time, my father still went on his drinking binges though raising less hell as he got older. One day, he made the mistake of getting belligerent with Mike Tracy. They started arguing outside the Lakeside, and just as my father turned to get in his car, he said something about Rod Tracy, Mike's father, who died of a fall when Mike was young. In two seconds of a heartbeat, Mike pulled his fist back and nailed my Dad smack in the nose yelling, "Don't you ever say anything about my father." My father apologized to Mike the next day and said he admired him for sticking up for his father. My Dad and Mike's Dad were actually very good friends. Secretly, I was elated, because my father deserved it, and now I knew I had a protector.

When Mike got angry, he was not violent. Instead, he would grumble, or yell, and then panic. This afforded me the opportunity to assert my will, get revenge, and infuriate him without fear of physical retaliation. One night, after leaving Big Moose Inn in Eagle Bay, I was designated to drive because I didn't drink that night; however, he took the keys from me insisting on driving. He was driving too fast on the old dirt road, so I asked him to slow down. Being a smartass, he slowed down to five miles an hour. I was exasperated and yelled, "For crying out loud, let me out of the car. I can walk faster."

"Really, you really want to get out?" he snapped back.

"That's what I said, didn't I. I'm not riding with you and getting killed. I didn't drink all night, so I could drive." "We agreed on that, and now you have to get all stupid and take the keys!"

"I'm not that drunk. I can drive!"

"Yes, you are, and no, you can't." "Stop the damn car now!" I yelled. He did. I got out and took off up the road. Soon, I heard the car coming back, so I ran into the woods, stepped in the lake, and got wet up to my knee. It was January and the temperature was well below freezing. Immediately, my pant leg froze. I watched the car go by as I hid behind a huge tree. He stopped the car, started hollering my name, and then drove back the way we came. I continued through the woods until I reached the main road. By now, Mike had gone up and down the road several times shouting my name. I hovered around the main road, running into the woods every time I heard his car. I never thought for one moment about freezing to death. I was completely comfortable in this environment in the woods between Eagle Bay and Long Lake.

Soon, I saw car lights, and knew immediately it was not our car. I jumped out into the road and flagged them down. It was the band from Big Moose Lodge and they lived in Long Lake. I told them Mike had left me and asked them for ride. They took me right to my house, where I promptly went to bed.

About 7:00 AM, Mike came in and woke me up, "Where in the hell have you been?"

"Right here asleep, I said. Where in the hell have you been?"

"Damn it, Gail, I woke everybody up in Raquette Lake looking for you. God, I thought you fell through the ice and drowned or something. How did you get here? Didn't you know I would come back?"

"No," I lied, "I didn't know you would come back, and I told you, I didn't want to ride with you. I rode home with the band."

"What?" He paced the floor shaking his head. We kissed, had wild sex and he soon learned not to say the words, "Then leave," to me because I would, no matter what the weather conditions were at the time. I would tell him, "Fine, I don't want to be with somebody who doesn't want me around," and I would be out the door. One time I slept in an old dump truck in Raquette Lake in 30 below zero weather because we were staying at Burke's cabins, got in a fight and he forgot and told me if I didn't like it to leave. Once again, he spent the rest of the night burning the road between Raquette and Long Lake while I watched from behind a tree in the safe black hollows of the forest.

Another pattern that continued with us is that I would still dump his clothes off at Burke's motel when he would disappear for days, or be unfaithful to me. My mother said she knew when she saw that red Dodge RT zoom by the restaurant loaded down with clothes, that Mike and I got into another fight.

He would wait a day or two until I calmed down, apologize, cry, and swear never to do it again and soon; Mom would see the red car returning loaded down with his clothes. I loved this man, and wanted a lifetime with him, but another love was already creeping up on us, a love that would wreak havoc on anyone or anything that got in its way.

148

CHAPTER 34

ANOTHER CAR WRECK

Mike and I drove like maniacs. We always had fast cars, and he always wrecked them, except for one, the one I wrecked on Blue Mountain hill. It was a winter night with new falling snow and once again, I was waiting for my man to come home. Around 2:00 AM, I started calling bars looking for him. I called a bar in Indian Lake and asked, "Is Mike Tracy there?"

The bartender replied, "Uh, is this Kathy?"

I was already furious and now I was steaming, "No, this is not Kathy," I screamed and slammed down the receiver. Bruce was staying overnight that night, so I ran in woke him up and told him I was leaving for a while. He looked up groggy eyed said okay and went back to sleep. I grabbed my keys and two bottles of beer from the refrigerator (I had already had several) and ran out the door. I jumped in my gold Duster that Mike had bought me to entice me to come back the last time, and spun out of the parking lot. By the time I flew by the Lakeside, I was hitting 80 mph, my mind dead set on storming into the bar and screaming at him to get out of my life. Fresh snow carpeted the road and shiny guardrails peaked through the four-foot snow banks like braces on teeth.

As I started up the backside of Blue Mountain hill, I drained the last beer. The next thing I remembered was hearing a loud thump, thump, thump noise. I opened my eyes and saw green tree branches whizzing by the passenger window. Suddenly, the car came to an abrupt stop. I opened the door and realized that I was on top of a snow bank, on top of the guardrail. Oh my God, I thought, I fell asleep. The cold air hit my face, sobering me up enough to realize I had to get out of the vehicle. It was perched precariously on top of the guardrail with a thirty-foot drop into the lake below. I jumped out my side of the car, landed in the road, and started walking down Blue Mountain Hill. The Town of Blue Mountain was even smaller than Long Lake, so finding anyone awake here, was going to be nearly impossible; however, just as I rounded the corner at the bottom of the hill, I saw Sedrick's old red truck parked on the side of the road. He was a drinking friend who frequented my father's bar and partied with our group. I trudged down the snowy road, walked up to the truck and looked in the window. Great, he was there. I banged on the window. He did not move. I thought, damn, he's out cold. I may not be able to rouse him. I banged harder and began to yell his name at the top of my lungs. After what seemed like an hour, he opened his eyes.

Sedrick unrolled the window, "Gail, what to hell?"

"I wrecked my car. It's up on the hill! I need help."

"You what?" He opened the door, got out, and asked again, "You wrecked the car? Are you all right?"

"Yes, yes, I'm fine, I replied, but my car, I think it's totaled!"

"Well, let's go up and see what we got. What in the hell are you doing out here at this time of night, uh morning anyway?"

"You don't want to know, and I don't want to tell you."

"Oh, Mike, he said shaking his head from side to side in a negative motion, say no more." We began walking up the hill to the car. In the Adirondacks, the last thing you ever did was call the police because people took care of things themselves; besides, the police could be miles away in another little town. If you ran into a snow bank, someone always had a truck or a chain and pulled you out. Tonight the police would not be called because I was drinking, so, Sedrick and I began the trek up the hill discussing what to do. We reached the scene, and realized that the only thing that saved me was the guardrail cable. It had wrapped around the axel preventing the car from going over the edge into the lake. We heard a car begin it's ascent up the hill. As the front end of the blue Chevelle came into view, we both realized that it was Mike. He saw my car on the snow bank, pulled over, got out, and immediately started yelling. "What to hell happened?

"She had an accident, you idiot," Sedrick said. They grew up together in houses on this hill, and they were good friends.

"Jesus, you've totaled this car," Mike muttered, as he walked around the car looking it over. "What to hell were you doing out here, anyway?"

"She was looking for your ass as usual," Sedrick replied.

"Get in. I'll take you home," Mike yelled, "Damn, and that car was new."

"For Christ sake, Mike, you could ask her if she's all right," Sedrick said. "She has blood on her mouth. Better make sure she's okay, you unfeeling bastard."

I was shaking by now. The alcohol was wearing off, and I was freezing. I heard Sedrick's comment about blood. Only then did I feel the pain in my mouth. I put my fingers to my lips and saw that they were blood stained.

As if awakened from a deep sleep, Mike put his arms around me, hugged me, and said, "I'm sorry for yelling at you, let me look at you." He checked my mouth, found a handkerchief in his car, and began wiping off the blood. "Looks like your teeth went through your lip." Come on, I'm taking you home. Sedrick, can you meet me in an hour? I'll get the grader (Mike drove the snow equipment for Raquette Lake) and pull her out?"

"Sure can, Man. See you then. We took him back to his truck, thanked him, and headed for home. Halfway home, I said, "Who in the hell is Kathy?"

CHAPTER 35

SUICIDAL

Kathy turned out to be my best friend's sister. Kathy turned out to be the woman who stopped by occasionally to have coffee with me. Kathy turned out to be the woman who tried to steal my man.

I left him again, and no matter how many times I left him, he always came back after each affair. There were other Kathy's, other excuses, other reasons for not coming home for three days, a week, a month until the effects of drinking a six pack a night, getting drunk on the weekends and being hopelessly in love with a womanizer plunged me into a six-month period of depression and attempted suicides. I convinced myself that my sister should raise my kids because I was a bad mother. I convinced myself that I should have been born in 1800s, that I was a mistake, and that the world would be a better place without me.

My first suicide attempt was with aspirin. I took 1000 of them. Bruce found the empty bottle and me passed out and called Mike. Mike found me, made me walk, eat burnt toast, and throw up. The whole night he was yelling about how my parents would think he did it, and have him arrested. I screamed back at him "You did do it; you made me fall in love with you, and then you screw anything that looks your way!" "I hate you; I hate you, just leave me alone, and let me die!" He didn't. I lived and when the acid in those aspirins hit my stomach, I was in agony for three days, temporarily lost my hearing, and knew I would not try to kill myself that way again.

Instead, the next time I chose a razor blade. Once again, Mike was leaving to get drunk or see his latest victim. I begged him to stay. He wouldn't. I felt so low, so degraded. What had happened to me? I had been an athlete, a cheerleader, a popular girl in my school. I won poetry-writing contests and could dance the pants off anyone. Where was that girl now? The bees stung and it hurt. That young girl so many years ago who was fearless, and ran wild and free as the wind was now in prison. I wanted more than ever to be free of this man, this torture, but my heart would not let go. I had no defense against his offense. I would pray that he would just leave and not come back, but he always did. God was never anywhere when you needed him. I prayed to die, I prayed for him to die, and we lived. I prayed for an answer and my answer was death. One night after Mike picked a fight so he could leave; I called my sister to baby sit, and took the kids to her house. I returned home, went into the bathroom, locked the door, took out a razor, and slashed my wrist horizontally then vertically. I cut many times, deeper and deeper until I saw red oozing out, then flowing like a faucet. I sat in the bathtub and waited to die.

Earlier, I wrote a suicide note to my children. I asked my sister to raise them, so they would have a father and a good mother. I looked away from the red on the tub, and closed my eyes. Than, I heard Mike's boot steps coming through the bedroom. He was walking very fast, and I saw the doorknob move. Then he pounded on the door, "Gail, open the damn door," he yelled. I said nothing. "Open this door right now or I'll bust it in." Again, I said nothing. There was a loud crack and there he was looming above me. "Jesus Christ, Gail," he whispered. He grabbed a towel, tied it around my wrist, grabbed another and tied it tight around my bicep, lifted me up, and carried me into the front seat of the truck. We raced like a fire engine to Tupper Lake Mercy General Hospital him yelling at me all the way, me in a stupor remembering that yelling sound and then nothing until I woke up in the emergency room. I opened my eyes and saw Dr. Lazar looking down at me. I heard Mike saying, "Jesus, Doc, if I hadn't felt like something was

154

wrong...I don't know, something just told me to go back." I looked down to my left and saw that Doc was working on my arm. Mike was pacing the floor and yelling, "God, Gail, I can't believe you did this," his voice getting louder as I came into full consciousness. In my state, it sounded like he was talking through a megaphone.

"Please, I whispered, get him away from me." I felt like everything was closing in on me. Mike's voice was getting, louder, and I wanted to pounce off that bed and beat him until he was raw or dead. Somebody needed to be gone—him or me.

Dr. Lazar said, "I think you should wait out in the waiting room, Mike." He immediately walked out of the room. I hated him. I glared at his back as he lumbered out the door.

"Gail, why did you do this?" Dr. Lazar asked.

"I cut it peeling an orange." I was always amazed at how fast a lie could fly off my tongue no matter what state I was in at the time.

"Uh huh, was the doctor's response, along with, "You know, missy, if you were trying to kill yourself, I would have to call social services."

"What?" I couldn't understand what he was saying, but I did hear kill yourself and social services, so once again I went with the peeling the orange story. "Dr Lazar, please don't lock me up." I begged. I tried to get up. "I'm not going to any Looney bin." "I'll leave right now. I didn't try to kill myself!" I shouted.

"Ok, ok, I won't call." Doc put his hand on my shoulder. It was a soft gentle touch and he whispered, "You just rest here and everything will be all right." Because he was a doctor and because his touch and his tone were so gentle, I believed him and did what he said. "The nurse will be in to check your vitals. It was then that I realized I was hooked up intravenously. "Young lady, you could have died tonight, so if I were you I would make some changes. Maybe you should ease up on the alcohol. You are too young to die. I can call and get you some help, someone to talk to if you want."

"I won't be put away?" I asked.

"No, I am going to leave information with Mike. I want you to call this counselor when you get home and set up an appointment."

"Ok, I whispered weakly, but will you tell Mike to stop yelling at me?"

"Yes, I can do that, Goodbye Gail," he said, as he turned to leave. I watched this wonderful white-haired man who probably saved my life again walk out the door. He never spoke of my suicide attempt again. He released me into Mike's care.

As I rode home from the hospital that night, I stared at the huge conifer trees jutting up to the sky on both sides of the road. I could not look at him. I felt safe in the black spaces between the giant trees. I imagined myself hiding there from everyone and everything under those massive marvels of the night. It was sometime during that ride that *The Voice* came to me. It was masculine, as clear as if I was face to face with a man having a conversation.

"Gail, no man is worth this." "No man is worth dying for," *The Voice* whispered as if telling me a secret and as suddenly as it was there, it was gone. I knew from that moment on that I would never attempt to take my life again, and I knew from that moment on that Mike Tracy and I were doomed if we stayed in Long Lake.

The next day, I gave Mike an ultimatum—we move to Elkton, Virginia where his brother lived, or he must leave.

Mike's answer was, "Hell no, I ain't moving down there."

"Ok, I said, then get your clothes; we are done." For the first time in the three years we had been together, my voice was strong. I knew this time that I meant it, and so did he.

"You're serious, aren't you?" he said looking at me as if he was seeing me for the first time.

"Oh, yes, I'm dead serious."

"I love you, Gail. I love Ricky and Monti, and I'm not losing the only family I've ever had. I am so sorry for everything. Mike was raised by an aunt and uncle because his mother was poor and needed help. They loved Mike and agreed to raise him. For a long time, he resented his mother for giving him away. He agreed to move to Virginia because he did not want to lose the only family he felt he ever had. He also promised he would be faithful and stop drinking.

Amazingly, for the first time, I did not believe him. I did not believe he would stop womanizing, and I did not believe he would stop drinking. Something in me had changed that night of the suicide. This change helped me to run away from danger; however, my will was still a force to be reckoned with, and it still kept me on the edge. Mike was telling the truth about moving, and in the spring of 1971, we landed in a trailer in Elkton, Virginia where we both quit drinking. I cooked in the little restaurant in front of the trailer at the bottom of Skyline Drive, and Mike drove heavy equipment during the day and worked nights for the owner of trailer. We were happy. Mike would take the boys with him in the evening on the bulldozer, and they began to love this wonderful man. Mike was a good provider and those winters in Elkton, after working all week excavating for the nuclear power plant in Charlottesville, he cut and sold wood in around Washington DC. Monti called him daddy, but Ricky still called him Mike.

One day Mike was playing with Ricky on the rug in the living room. He was tickling him and rolling around the floor with him. It was time to stop and Mike told him to go get his pajamas on, Ricky said, "Ok, Daddy," and scampered off to his room. Mike looked at me smiling as if he had just won the lottery. I put my finger to my mouth in the shush signal and we went in the bedroom where I told Mike it was best not to make a big deal about it right now. He was as excited as I had ever seen him and within a month, Mike was Daddy to both my boys, and he strutted around with them bragging to anyone who would listen to him about his sons. He was a caring father and a hard worker and life was good. I began to think that our little family was going to make it. We were Ozzie and Harriet. Ricky was playing t-ball and doing great in 1st grade. For the first time since having the boys, I did not work. I spent time with the boys, cooked wonderful meals, and baked creative cakes. I loved my life. No bees would ever sting me again.

Mike, Monti, Ricky, Elkton, VA

CHAPTER 36

TWO SCHOOLS AND A TRAGEDY

We moved several times in Virginia, and each place was a new little town, so the children went to two different schools. They started out in Elkton; then we bought the trailer and moved to Mcgaheysville a few miles away. Next, we found a park with a few trailers, ours an end unit surrounded by a large field. It gave the boys a field to play in, and I liked the small park; however, this property was sold and we had to find a new place. Our last move in the trailer was in a lovely park across from the Merck Vitamin plant in Elkton. Many mornings, the smell of chemicals wafted through the air, but the owner of this park had horses, and the boys did not have to change schools. There were trees in this park, so I loved it. We had baseball games with the whole community joining in and the boys made friends with the children in the next trailer.

In February of 1974, we received horrible news. We learned that a fire broke out in Ricky's friend, Charlie Bean's, house on Kickerville Road in Long Lake. It was a cold winter night and Patty, Richard, and the children had gone to bed. Richard and Patty woke up to a room full of smoke. Pat was pregnant at the time. Richard told her jump out the window and he would get the kids. She hesitated, so he pushed her out the second floor window, turned to go get Charlie and Kathy, and immediately went straight through the floor. Pat landed in the snow, got up and ran around to the front trying to get up the stairs. She severely burned her hands and neck, but lived through it. Richard, Charlie, and Kathy died that night, and two days later Pat gave birth to a little girl, she named Faith. I debated whether to tell Ricky and decided it was better for him to hear it from his mother than from someone else. He was nine years old. He understood, and we cried together for our friends.

CHAPTER 37

NEW FRIENDS AND RELATIVES

Mike and I started drinking again after two years of being sober. One day Mike came home and said he wanted to visit a friend who lived in Winchester, VA. Two weeks later, we all headed to Winchester for the weekend. Friday night, Mike and I sat at the bar with Snow and his wife drinking cokes while they drank mixed drinks. By midnight, we had surrendered, got drunk, puked the next morning, talked about the great time we had and vowed to come back in couple of weeks. From that weekend on, I was off and running with my old love, alcohol. I only drank on weekends; however, I began to notice that many of these nights, everyone passed out or went to bed but me. I did not go to sleep. Instead, I drank until I passed out. I liked drinking at home because it was cheaper, and I could stay up all night. Conversely, Mike liked drinking in bars, getting in fights, and chasing women. Since I had the kids and Mike was so jealous, going to bars was not an option for me.

A year after we moved to Elkton, my brother, Mike and his wife, Sherry, and their baby, Tracy, moved to Harrisonburg, VA. Sherry and I immediately became best friends while Mike Tracy and Mike Huntley continued being drinking friends. Many nights, the guys went out carousing around in Harrisonburg leaving Sherry and I stranded at home. I would get drunk and talk this poor patient woman's head off about how I was leaving Mike because he was nothing but a drunk. I loved Sherry, admired her, and wished I were more like her. She was pretty, petite, intelligent, thoughtful, and didn't drink; all the things I was not.

I remember always wishing I were somebody else. I was jealous of my sister because she was beautiful. I was jealous of people who scored higher grades than I did. I was never satisfied to be just one of the herd. If I was not the best cheerleader or team member, then I was the worst, and I never felt good enough or like I belonged anywhere. I wanted more in life. I wanted to go to college and be a better person. I still tried hard to be good like Sherry, but I was not successful. My children forced me to grow up in many ways, but I saw myself as a fallen angel with no life skills and no intelligence.

I did manage to attend a business school in Harrisonburg, VA, and graduated with a Secretarial of Science degree. My grades were high, but I rationalized the reason for this was because this was an easy school designed to get your money so they gave you good grades. I knew I was not capable of earning those scores. I got a job at Dunham Bush as an Administrative Assistant and loved the people I worked with, especially a girl who became my friend. I was delighted to make a friend and began playing tennis with her. Mike was jealous of her, called her a tramp, and ordered me to stop seeing her. When I suggested that he had no reason not to trust me, he responded, "but you are easily swayed." I knew from that remark that Mike did not know me. Men never knew me, and that always cut deep. I wanted this man to see me but jealousy and fear blinded him.

CHAPTER 38

STEALING TREES AND STEALING HEARTS

Mike had a job clearing a large site not far from Elkton. I missed the Adirondacks, and I wanted two little pine trees to plant on each side of the steps, so I asked him to bring two pine trees home from his job. He kept forgetting, and I kept nagging him about my trees.

One night on a drunk with my brother, they decided to get me a tree. They went to Harrisonburg and Mike Tracy got out, grabbed a potted tree from in front of the bank, and tried to push it into my brother's blue Cobra. They realized that the tree was too large, so Mike Tracy, being the nice guy that he was, decided to return it to the bank. While he was carrying this tree back to the bank, the Harrisonburg police come around the corner. They arrested them and took them to jail. As usual, Mike and my brother had used the ruse of leaving to purchase cigarettes in order to go out on the town, leaving Sherry and I stranded at home with three kids. At around 3:00 AM, the telephone rang. We looked at each, "Mike's in jail again, and I'll be damned if I'm bailing him out," I said. Sherry bailed my brother out, but I refused to pay Mike's way out, so his brother, Pat, paid the bail. The next day, there was a big write up in the Harrisonburg paper about the "Shrub Thieves."

Hurting became a way of life for me. As with Kenneth, I lay alone in bed listening for the tire sounds to alert me that Mike was home. I loved this man but gradually the drinking, going to jail, womanizing, and jealousy took its toll. I knew Mike loved us, but I also knew I wanted more in life. I was sick of being controlled, I could not tolerate one more infidelity, and I wanted to go to college, but he would not allow it. At this time, I had enrolled Ricky in Little League in Elkton. Monti and I went to all his practices and games; however; Mike did not like watching sports, so he stayed home. A woman named Linda moved in three trailers down from us and immediately began flirting with Mike. He was a handsome sexy man with a boyish smile. There was nothing not to like about his looks. I had tried several times to leave him, but he would cry and beg me to stay with promises never to do it again. Each time, my heart would melt, my brain would tell me he would change, and I would stay.

In 1975, after one more infidelity, I told him that if he cheated on me again, that was it; I was taking the kids and leaving. I wanted freedom. I wanted out of this prison, and I was willing to go to any lengths to get it. Hence, I devised a plan involving Linda and Mike.

I began my plan by doing what I always did, taking Monti and Ricky to the ball field leaving Mike home alone. I no longer begged him to go, too. Next, I invited Linda over for dinner and cards a couple of nights. One evening Mike said, "Linda and Ted, our other neighbor, are coming over and we are going to play poker while you're at the game."

"Oh, that's great," I said, thinking, here we go. By the next week, they were playing cards most evenings I was gone. I felt strong and excited because my plan was working. Soon, Mike would not come home at all one night and then I had him and my guiltless way out. Two weeks later on a Saturday night, I lay awake at 2:00 Am because Mike was not home. After his last drunk driving ticket, he had promised that if he were drinking too much, he would not drive home. He would pull over on the side of the road, sleep it off, and then come home. I naively told him that I accepted that. He happily agreed to that plan since it gave him the whole night to sleep around. Well, I wasn't naïve anymore, so at 4:30 AM, I got up, snuck over to Linda's trailer, and saw Mike's truck in the driveway. At first, I felt the familiar pain, but I stopped it in its tracks and thought how stupid and arrogant he was to park smack dab in the middle of her driveway with me two driveways down.

I knew his plan was to get up early, come home and tell me he had drank too much and parked along the road somewhere. I went back home and waited. At around 5:30 AM, he walked through the door and began his story, "Gail, I am so sorry, but I did pull over on the side of road like you asked me to and slept a couple of hours, so I wouldn't get another DUI."

I smugly snapped back, "You're a damn liar. You idiot, God, Mike, do you really think I am that stupid?"

"No, what are you talking about?" "That was the plan and I did what you asked, so what to hell are you so mad about?"

"I am mad because the side of the road last night was Linda's driveway." "I walked up there and saw your truck."

"You what?" "You went up their checking up on me?"

I did not take the, "It's your fault bait" this time. Instead I declared," Yes I did, and we are done." "She is the last one, Mike," "I'm leaving." The crying started. The begging started. The lying continued and soon he gave up because he could no longer take me to guilt. Freedom overshadowed guilt like the northern lights eclipse the night sky. Hope was erased making room for truth.

"But, where will you go?" "You can't just take the kids away from me."

"Oh yes I can. What kind of role model are you for them? I've already rented an apartment in Harrisonburg," I said as I went in the bedroom and began breakfast for the boys.

"You what?" "How could you behind my back…"

"No, Mike, this is your fault and yours alone. I love you, but I want out, and I am out. You can stay here with your latest conquest."

He walked out the door, got in his truck, and drove away. I packed all of our things, pulled out of the driveway by 3:00 PM that afternoon, and glanced back once before I turned the corner onto the main road. The boys were sad, and I felt horrible for them, but I knew I had to leave. Mike moved into our trailer with Linda and stuck me paying $500.00 toward what we owed on it. I still loved him, and my heart shattered in pieces whenever I saw them together. The sadness in my boys' eyes tore through me like wind cutting through my soul. Did I do the right thing? I felt like no one thought so but me, but I landed a second job at J C Penny's, went to work, enrolled the kids in the new school and began to enjoying playing football in the front yard with my boys and strolling down to a little bar called The Elbow Room.

CHAPTER 39

BACK TO LONG LAKE

'One night at the bar, I began a conversation with a handsome a blonde haired blue-eyed man named Connor. We swapped our losing man losing woman stories and soon began dating. He sang and played guitar beautifully, and we spent many nights at his parents' house playing music with relatives. I loved their country home and began going with him when my brother and his wife would baby sit. He was a kind gentle man, but I hesitated introducing him to my children. I was not sure how I felt about him, and I still grieved over Mike. One night, after the kids were asleep, I invited Connor over to watch television with me. He had just taken his boots off and put his feet on the footstool. Suddenly, we heard a loud bang on the door and a man yelled, "Who you got in there?"

"Oh my God, it's Mike," I whispered to Connor.

"The one you left in Elkton."

"Yes, and he's mad." "How does he know you're here?"

"He must be watching you, he said. Well, come on, let the guy in." He got up and started putting his boots on.

"No, Connor, you don't know him." Although Mike had never hit me, he would hit another man in a second.

"Gail, you either let me in now or I'm busting this door down," Mike yelled as he banged on the door again.

"Connor, I whispered, take your boots, and hide in the kitchen, when he comes through the door at me, you run out.

"But, I ain't…."

"No, I can't have the kids waking up to two men in fight." "Please, do what I ask."

"Okay, but I don't like it," he said as he went around the corner and crouched behind the kitchen wall. I headed for the door to unlock it, heard Mike's foot slam against it and stepped back just in time for the door to miss me by inches. I was terrified when I saw Mike's face as he took two huge steps toward me. Out of the corner of my eye, I saw Connor slip out the door. Mike pushed me down on the couch. "Who the hell was up here?"

"None of your business!" I spit back, as we both heard Connor's footsteps pounding down the stairs. We raced to the window, looked out and there he was running down the road, barefoot carrying his boots.

"There he is, Mike shouted, and by God, he won't live to come up here again!" He raced out the door flying down the steps. I sat on the couch trembling in fear thankful the children were sleeping through this mess. A few minutes later, I heard him climbing back up the stairs. I was furious and fearful.

He came back winded and much calmer. I blasted him with "Who do you think you are? Should I call Linda and tell her what you did?" "Damn it, Mike, leave me alone! You chose her and you can't tell me who I can see. I need to get on with my life too."

He said, "I know. I made a huge mistake. I love you and my boys. I am so sorry. I don't blame you for leaving. I don't know why I did those things to you when you were so good to me. I won't bother you again, Gail, but if you ever change your mind, call me." We talked a few more minutes. I agreed to let him see the kids when he wanted, and ten minutes after he left, the police arrived. I lied for him and told the police someone broke in. Later the police found out I lied, and the proprietor evicted me. I avoided Connor out of embarrassment, and I ended up paying for all the damages to the apartment. Such was the way of my world—many times; I lied for my man and ended up left with the baggage I had created.

This event led me to quitting my job and moving back to Long Lake with my parents where I got job in Albany at RCA and lived with Charlie and Sharon Palmer, friends from Long Lake. During the week, the boys stayed with my Mom and Dad. They were now eight and nine years old and we had never been apart for even one night, so on Sunday nights when I had to leave for Albany, they would scream and cry. Ricky would grab onto my arm and beg me not to go. It was horrible. I hurt so bad, that I cried all the way to Albany. I cried in my bed every night. Finally, after about a month of this, one Sunday night on the way to Albany, I decided I could not do this one more week. A plan began to form in my mind and first thing Monday morning I called RCA, told them my grandmother died, packed up all my clothes, and went back to my kids, never returning to that job.

The boys and I danced around the house in joy when I told them I was not going back. I got a low paying job in Long Lake at a small business owned by a man who sold bait and built houses. The boys joined the scouts and played baseball. My parents were now caretakers at Lake Eaton State Park, so my sister, Sheryl, and the kids, and I lived in their house they had built on Dock Road beside the big house where I grew up.

Sheryl and I smoked pot, drank beer, and went barhopping when Venita or Mom would baby-sit. Venita lived next door, which presented one big problem with this set up— her husband was a state trooper. I remember being scared that Conway would smell the marijuana and come and arrest me. We hid the pot in the ceiling tile in Sheryl's bedroom. One time after I had smoked, I left the bag on the table. Apparently, Ricky saw Conway coming up the path to the house, so he grabbed the bag of pot and hid it. At ten years old, this beautiful intelligent boy took on the role of protecting a mother living on the edge of reality.

Of course, I was not aware of my addiction to dangerous situations, alcohol, fast cars, and dares, but I loved them all. I drank more than other people did, I loved more than other people did, and I drove faster than other people did. That is how I lived and how I thought. I professed to love my children more than life, yet my child was breaking the law for me. In my heart, they were gold, but in my actions, they were tin. I made decisions based on me, and talked about decisions based on them. One of those decisions led me straight into the arms of a man who sold pot, drank Budweiser, and had once vowed to marry me.

CHAPTER 40

STEWART

I called him Turtle. It was the way I taunted him because he had a recessed chin. I flirted with him because I had control. I knew he had loved me for a long time. He was older than I was, had a pot garden, and hid the harvested pot in the chandeliers of his trailer on Cedarlands Park in Long Lake, NY. Stewart was a Navy man, soon to be released into retirement. I met him again in the Lakeside while drinking beer and playing pool. This time, I was 30 and he was 40. He made me laugh. He took my boys fishing and taught them how to shoot a bow, and arrow. Cedarland Park had once housed the Walker family, a wealthy family who lived there in the early 1900s. James Walker built a magnificent log mansion and several other structures around Rock Pond, guarded at the entrance by a unique stone gatehouse. When James died, his sister inherited it and when she died, her employee, Watts, inherited the gatehouse. Now, it was Cedarlands Boy Scout camp, and when Stewart retired from the Navy, he became caretaker of this vast reserve.

This man with turquoise eyes, hook nose and red hair, was the kind of man who became handsome with a stare, not a glance. The story, though not from him, was that his father abused him, so his uncle and aunt took him in and raised him as their son. All I remembered of him from elementary school was that he offered me a seat on the school bus when most high school boys didn't do that. He laughed all the time, and I heard stories about his drinking and fighting with the local boys. When he graduated, he and went into the Navy. He was home on leave the night we met at Tom Toms when I was 13 and he proposed to me. Now, I was a woman and a mother and we met again. He had served several years in Vietnam and his eyes carried a sadness that I wanted to make go away. He loved the woods and we tramped through Cedarlands together with his dog, Dublin, the smartest dog I ever knew. Dublin would walk into a bar with Stewart, stand on his hind legs with his paws on the bar, and whine for a Slim Jim or Polish Sausage. He would get it, then lie down under a table or go out in the truck and wait for Stewart. Soon, it was Dublin and I racing through the woods playing hide and seek. He always found me, and I fell in love with that beautiful dog.

Stewart and I began dating, meaning we met at a bar and drank together, or we went to his trailer, drank, and smoked pot together. Sometimes we all went fishing and sometimes he spent time with the boys. They liked him because he was good to them. One night, they brought back a few trout from Big Brook where they had been fishing. Stewart cleaned them and cooked them. He knew we did not like fish. I made hot dogs and salad. I watched as Stewart came over and plopped a trout on Ricky's plate. Ricky looked up at me. I said, "You know, he doesn't like fish."

"What do you mean, he doesn't like fish. I cooked it for him and he's going to eat it," he snapped.

My breathing stopped abruptly. I stared at him for a few seconds just as Ricky repeated, "But, I don't like fish."

"I don't give a damn what you like, you're eating the fish I cooked!" Stewart yelled.

I jumped up from the table, throwing my fork down. "Like hell he is," I yelled back, who do you think you are, telling my son what he will or will not eat?" "Well, don't worry about it because, we're leaving!" With that, the boys got up and followed me out the door, Stewart right behind us.

"Hey, I'm sorry. Don't leave. I didn't know," he stammered.

I stared at him with angry eyes "Go to Hell, and don't ever come around me again," I screamed as I jumped in the car, slammed the door, and raced out the driveway, stones and dust spewing behind me. I looked in the rearview mirror at the boys in back. They were sad. It felt like a giant fist grabbed my heart, and began squeezing it tighter and tighter. Tears welled up in my eyes. "I am sorry boys, I am so sorry." I love you."

"It's ok, Mom," Ricky said.

"I love you, Mom," Monti whispered.

For the average sensible woman, this would have been the end of that blossoming romance, but it was not. Perhaps I was drawn to the insanity like a moth to fire. Perhaps I only saw what I wanted to see, or I forgave and forgot too quickly. Whatever the reason, he wooed me with I'm sorry, I miss you, I love the boys, several bunches of flowers, and two new books. Stewart and I were avid readers—another thing we had in common besides the woods, pot, and beer. He loved Louis La'Amour books, and he wore me down with his warm smile and kindness to my boys.

We were married on a cool September day in Long Lake. The reception was at the Lakeside Lodge. During the week, we stayed around Cedarlands, walking through the woods, going to the lodge on the lake, shooting guns, playing classical music, and reading. Stewart got up early every morning and took the boys out past the gatehouse to catch the school bus. We lived in a wonderland. Many evenings, when I got off work and began the trek back on the dirt road to our house, I saw black bear cubs, fox, deer, pheasant, and many other beautiful animals. On the weekends, we usually went out on Friday or Saturday night. Dublin would stand guard on the chair by the door ready to pounce on anyone who tried to enter. The kids fell in love with this dog, and she fell in love with them. Her top priority became protecting them.

One of Stewart's duties as caretaker included checking on some old camps on the East side of the long dirt road that ran parallel to Long Lake. Early one morning, we grabbed our coffee, hopped in the truck, and poked along the ruddy road until we reached a driveway on the East side. Stewart pulled in and parked in front of an old red barn. He got out and said, "Come on, I want to show you something." I got out and we walked past a couple of other buildings until we reached a round structure with a large board across the top of it. A few steps away from this one, there was another similar structure. "Those are wells, he said, probably built by the first families that came here.

"Really, I said becoming increasingly interested, can we look inside? Do you think there is still water down there?"

"Probably, but I don't want to take the boards off. They are on there for safety reasons, so no one can fall in."

I shuddered. "That would be horrible." This property was miles from civilization, and I thought how frightening it must have been at night in the early 1800s, when the men had to be away for a few nights leaving the women and children to fend for themselves. I began to back away from the well and said, "Well, what do you have to do down here?"

"Hey, look," Stewart said, as he lifted one of the boards off the well, you can see down there now. "You want to look?"

"Uh, no, not anymore, it's kind of creepy."

"For Christ's sake, Gail, it's just an old well." "Come on just take a look."

I thought, how stupid to be scared. He's right. It's just a well. I walked over and peered into the dark abyss. "I can't see anything, but I can hear the water."

"Right, he said, putting his arm around me, so now you know there is still water down there. Now, young lady, I have work to do, so I had better quit sightseeing with you and get back to it."

"Okay, Dublin and I are going to walk around, just holler when you are done." We gave each other a hug and kiss, and I took off down to the lake. As Stewart went about his work, I sat on a rock gazing up at the sun filtering through the pines

174

and hardwoods making patterns on the grass. It was a crisp fall morning, and I loved this mysterious place filled with forest sounds steeped in Long Lake history.

"Gail, Gail, I'm done here." "Let's go. Hey, you okay?" He was looking down at me quizzically.

"What?" "Oh, sure, you startled me." "It is just so beautiful down here," I said coming back to reality.

Stewart put his arm around me, and kissed me on the cheek. "Yes, I love it here too, especially with you in it." "I sure wouldn't mind spending the rest of my days here."

"Me neither," I said as I hugged him and we walked arm and arm back to his vehicle. All of Cedarlands Park was magnificent to me. I loved to hear the cawing crows, the boreal chickadees with their scratchy chick a dee dee dee and the melodic canary sounds of the sparrows. All was abuzz in the forest getting ready for winter. The brook was full now from autumn rain. The air smelled of damp moss from the water worn rocks permeated the air. Soon, we were back home reading our books and making house-building plans.

A week later when we were up at the great camp on Rock Pond, I heard the haunting sound of loons on the clear sapphire lake. I pointed, "Look, Stewart, there are two of them." They were lovers, and I loved watching them glide out around each other and then bob under and back up. They were amazing to watch.

Out of the corner of my eye, I saw Stewart lift his gun to shoot out toward the lake. He loved to shoot and did so regularly to keep his expert status intact. I figured he was shooting at some target he had set up on a tree at the edge of the woods. I wasn't paying much attention because I was so enamored by the antics of the two magnificent loons. The shot rang out, and one of the loons immediately went under. I realized, the noise had scared them. I turned to Stewart and said, "Do you have to shoot that gun when the loons are out?" "The noise is scaring them."

"Well, they ought to be scared since their getting shot at." He looked at me as if I was crazy.

"What?" I glanced at him and then stared out at the water only then seeing black liquid floating on the surface. "Oh my God, you killed, you shot that loon?" I gasped.

"They eat all my fish," he replied, putting the gun in the truck.

I couldn't believe my eyes, "But, they weren't hurting you." "They were a pair, lifelong partners," I replied almost in tears.

He walked over to me. "Gail, there are plenty of loons on this lake and one less is not going to make a difference. They bring the boy scouts up here to fish and as caretaker, I am supposed to make sure they have fish to catch."

"But you stock it," I argued. I had been with Stewart when the truck came in, and they filled the pond with fish.

"Right and we didn't stock it for loons or ducks." I said a prayer for that lovely creature, and cringed when I wondered how many other loons he had killed.

Stewart started the truck, put it in gear and we slowly rumbled up the little dirt road and down the driveway to the silver trailer plopped right in the middle of this wonderful woodland. I remained quiet all night. I could not get the vision of that poor unsuspecting loon gliding gracefully over that lovely lake with its mate one minute and the next, toppling over like a plastic duck in a carnival shooting game. The next morning I asked Stewart not to shoot any more loons. He said he did not know it would upset me that way and promised not to do it again. I finally rationalized that he had been in Vietnam killing people, so killing a loon was nothing to him. Perhaps he was doing his job, and I appreciated that he would not kill any more for me. Our lives moved on without incident. We were in love. The boys were in scouts with Stewart taking them fishing, buying them school clothes and falling in love with all of us.

176

CHAPTER 41

NIGHTMARE

'On a cold December evening, I met Stewart for drinks after work at the Lakeside Lodge. We had a couple of drinks and arrived home around 11:00 AM. Stewart immediately noticed that it was warm in the house. He walked over, looked at the thermostat, and bellowed, "Who turned up the heat?" Ricky and Monti were in their bedroom and the house was silent. Stewart yelled again, "Answer me, which one of you turned up the heat?"

My head snaps around. My body comes to attention and I see the shadow cross his face. I know that shadow. It is the face of insanity. I saw it change lightning fast in my father and in Kenneth. Now, fear rips through me as I realize that it is back. Stewart starts to stomp down the hallway to the bedroom. I grab him.

"Stewart, just turn it down." My voice cracks. He pushes me aside and rams into the boy's room.

"One of you better answer me," he shouts again. I hear both boys saying, "It wasn't me." Then Ricky says, "It wasn't us." By the time I get into the bedroom, Stewart has his fist twisted around Ricky's shirt and is lifting him into the air. Stewart is roaring, "You're lying." "You ain't going to lie to me!" Oh my God, I think, he is going to hit Ricky.

Frantically, I rush through the bedroom doorway past him and wedge myself between him and Ricky. This forces him to drop Ricky. My face is within inches of his red face, and I scream at him, "Don't you ever put your hands on my child again!" "I turned your Goddamn thermostat down; I did it!" I screamed. By now, hot anger is gushing through me like molten lava. Nobody touches my kids, nobody. I stomp down the hallway and begin to pull my clothes out of the drawers. "I'm not staying with you, I yell, you're crazy!" Suddenly, hands grab my arm, and spin me around. I feel a hot stinging slap on my face, once then twice. He pushes me so hard on my shoulders with both his hands that my feet fly upward, and I smash to the floor on my back.

"You're not going anywhere," he says in a low calm controlled voice. His foot is resting on my stomach. I am terrified. I look up at him, as he sits down on my stomach. Air gushes from my mouth. The face I see is not the one I married. This face is rust red, pinched up causing his eyes to become slits. His fist cracks into my jaw with such force that my head snaps to one side, and I feel my nose hit the floor. I see his fist go up again. I watch it come down. When I regain consciousness, I am sprawled across the bed. I open my eyes and see that it is still dark outside. A moan escapes my throat bringing boot steps and more beatings. I wake up and Stewart is shaking me, "Wake up." "The boys need breakfast, and then I'm taking them to school." I feel like I am swimming up through layers of water trying to get to the top. "Come on; come on," he says. The tone in his voice is steady, and I began to think I am having a bad dream until I try to get up. I cannot, so he helps me up. I come out to the kitchen. The boys look at me, and their faces go white. Stewart looks at the clock. "Hey, it's 7:25." "Hurry up, boys, we'll be late."

Ricky says, "I need my school books, just a minute." He leaves and comes into the living room with the shotgun pointed at Stewart and says, "Leave my mother alone or I'll blow your head off!"

"Ricky, no," I caution. "Don't. It will be okay. You just need to go to school. Please, honey, put the gun down." I am scared Stewart will grab it and the gun will fire, or Ricky will actually shoot this man and have to live with it. Stewart takes the gun from him and holds onto it. Frantically, my mind kicks into gear--I think, they can't come back here! He is ushering them out

178

the door. I try to think, and then I plead, "Stewart, please, let me hug them good by,"

He stops, contemplates, and then instructs them, "Okay, boys, go hug your mother."

Both boys hug me, and I whisper in Ricky's ear, "Go to Aunt Venita's." I watch them go out the door, stealing one last look at me before closing the door. Stewart reopens the door, turns to me, looks at the phone, and rips it straight off the wall. Before he shuts the door again, he looks back at me and sneers, "I'll be back for you." "You're going down the well."

"For God's sake, Stew," I begin, and he slams the door shut.

I spring into action as soon as the red Ford turns right at the end of the driveway. I stumble out the door, run to the gray car, jump in, and realize, to my horror, that he took the keys and the CB radio. I know I only have about ten minutes to escape. It will take him ten minutes to bring the kids out to Spenglers' house on Kickerville Road where they catch the bus. My mind races, my only chance is to run through the woods and get to town before he finds me. I run down the driveway, across the road, and straight to the waters edge. I know this is the shortest route out of here. I think, I can swim across and get to my Dad's house. I am a strong swimmer and I have swum across this lake hundreds of times. Then I heard, *The Voice*. It says, "The lake is too cold. You don't know how badly you are hurt. Go by land."

I begin running like a frightened deer over rotting logs, back across the road away from the lake, through brush toward Big Brook swamp. I hear the truck coming back up the road. I run faster. If I can just get to the gatehouse, Spengler's house is within shouting distance of the gatehouse. I am gasping for breath but know I am close. I know that soon I will see the intricate iron bars of the gatehouse. I come to the opening and my eyes strain to see the black iron gate. Instead, I am staring straight at the silver trailer through trees. My God, how can I be back here? I know I went in the right direction. Then, I see something else that makes my blood run cold. I see Stewart, walking into the woods with his gun over his shoulder. I am so close I can hear him humming. I glance fervently back over my shoulder. He is coming at a steady pace, as if in a trance. Oh, my God, I realize that he is hunting me! Immediately, I spin around and run crashing through the woods like a wild, wounded bear. I am sailing through the woods, not looking back. I run in the opposite direction even though it feels like this is the wrong way. I jump the bank into Big Brook swamp heading south this time. Soon, I am thigh deep in mud. It is exhausting pulling one foot up from the mire and putting the next one down. It takes all my strength.

I am lying on the side of the road with my cheek on the dirt. I hear whistling.

He picks me up, and soon I am in the passenger's side of the truck. I don't remember how I got to the truck. I assume he must have carried me. I see the shotgun standing between us. He is driving down the dirt road whistling and humming as if we are on a Sunday afternoon drive.

"Stewart, please take me home. What are you doing? What is the matter with you?"

"With me, nothing is the matter with me. I told you, I'm putting you in the well."

"My God, Stewart, you can't kill me, I'm your wife." "Don't you think my family will miss me?" The whistling continues. I grab the gun. He looks over at me, reaches in his pocket, pulls out two shotgun shells, and gives me a sardonic smile. He does not speak. I do not want to die, and that horrific dark well terrifies me. My mind searches frantically for a way out, and when Stewart slows down to round the next curve, I jump out and start running. He stops the truck and continues methodically walking toward me, never rushing, never running. I fall down, fighting the blackness enveloping me. He grabs me by

180

the collar and drags me back to the truck. I know I am dead. "Please Stewart, I beg, shoot me now. Kill me now instead of in the well." He puts me back in the truck. I keep thinking I can get through to him because I can't believe I am going to die. Stewart, think about it, you will go to jail for the rest of your life. You won't get away with it. You love me, Stewart." He continues on his mission to the well humming the whole time. At times, I think that maybe this is death, so I remain quiet. Then, I know I am alive, so I plead, beg, and reason as I pass out and awaken again. Nothing moves him from his task.

Somewhere on that road, I stop struggling, my body goes limp, and I accept my fate. At that moment, I feel weightless. Light surrounds me. *The Voice* whispers, "You will be okay." I slip out of consciousness. Now, I open my eyes and see my heels making drag marks on the ground. He is pulling me through the woods by my collar. I search the recesses of my mind and pray for my boys who will grow up without me. I hear his breathing and see the sun filtering through the leaves, splattering my boot trail with fractured light.

Bump, bump, bump, falling. I'm falling. My head is slamming against a wall. It makes a loud knocking sound as it bounces off the object. I open my eyes and see trees. Oh my God, there are trees in Heaven, I think. I turn my head and there he is. I realize that my head is hitting the truck window. I'm not dead. I am confused. I do not dare to say anything. Soon, I see the trailer come into view. I feel Stewart lift me in his arms and carry me up the steps. He places me on the couch, goes to the sink, washes his hands, turns around, walks into the living room, looks at me, and mutters, "Oh my God, what have I done, what to hell have I done?" He races out the door, and I hear the truck speeding down the driveway. I close my eyes still not sure, if I will live. I do not care. I sleep.

Around 6:00 that night, I awoke to a vehicle coming up the driveway. My body froze. I was still on the couch.

Sometimes I saw the couch on the ceiling. Sometimes I saw table on the ceiling, but it all seemed normal to me. I slipped in and out of consciousness all day. Hearing the vehicle, I dragged myself up off the couch and stood in the doorway holding onto the doorsills. It was my sister's husband, Conway, the state trooper. The police car scared me. He got out of the car, stood by the driver's side window, and yelled, "Are you okay?"

"Yes, I'm fine," I shouted back.

"The kids said you were hurt." It was dark and he could not see me. "Are they supposed to spend the night?"

"No, I'm all right, yes, they spend the night," I shouted back, holding myself up now leaning against the doorframe.

"Ok, but did you and Stewart have a fight?"

"No," I said. I didn't remember us fighting. The police car was now floating in the air, and I was going to vomit, but I had no cognitive understanding that anything was wrong with me.

"Ok then, I'll see you tomorrow." He got in the car and rolled up the window and left. I went back to my conscious/unconscious world on the couch. Stewart came home reeking of alcohol around 8:00 PM, and passed out in the recliner.

Conway went home and told my sister I was okay, but Venita could not sleep that night. She had found the kids at the ball diamond after school that day. Even though I had told Ricky to go to Aunt Venita's, Stewart told them to go to the ball diamond after school, and he would pick them up there. After what they witnessed that morning, they were not about to disobey him. Venita saw them at the ball diamond at 5:30 PM, went to investigate and that is when they told her we had a fight and Stewart hit me, hence, she took them to her house and sent Conway up to check on me.

As soon as the kids were off to school the next morning, Venita got in the car and drove to Cedarlands. She came straight through the door, took one look at me on the couch, and drove me to Tupper Lake Hospital. Stewart had fractured my skull in the frontal sinus area. The doctors prescribed enormous amounts of penicillin to prevent infection to my brain. I had a broken jaw and many other injuries that would plague me for years to come including Post Traumatic Stress Syndrome, which caused me to shake so violently I thought I would die.

My sister took care of me. Conway advised me not to charge Stewart, as it would involve many court visits and much interrogation, and he didn't think I could handle it. The surgeon wanted me to charge him, so he could not harm anyone else. I did not charge him because I could only escape and try to erase this nightmare from my mind. When my physical injuries healed, I moved into trailer on the North Point Road in Long Lake, where he stalked me, so I moved further away to Saranac Lake, where he continued to stalk me.

CHAPTER 42

AND THE WALLS CAME TUMBLING DOWN

I had a mental breakdown in Saranac Lake, NY. I secured a job tending bar at the Swinging Tiger and rented an apartment above it. My sister, Sheryl, moved in with me. She was a beautiful girl with natural blonde hair, big blue eyes, and the biggest heart imaginable. We became very close, but now we began smoking pot, taking pills, and drinking almost every night. My physical wounds from Stewart healed; my emotional wounds ran rampant. My mother knew I was not well, but I did not understand the apprehension I saw in her eyes when she looked at me. My Mom knew things, and she knew I was not well.

One afternoon, as I was pouring a drink for one of the regular customers who was seated at the end of the bar, I heard the door swing open. A man walked toward the back and sat down at the table against the wall. When I finished pouring Rick his drink, I turned around to see who came in. I thought, that looks like…. It was. It was Stewart. Instantly, my body began to vibrate and my throat constricted. I was in a panic. What do I do? I pretended to wash glasses and ignore him, but Rick said, "Uh, Gail, you've got a customer over there." He pointed and I followed his lead staring straight into Stewart's eyes. I had to go. It was my job, so I went to the table.

"What are you doing here, Stewart?"

"Hey, I don't want any trouble. I'm not even drinking. I want a coke. I want to talk to you."

"Well, I don't want to talk to you," I snapped as I walked away. I poured him a coke and set it down in front of him.

"Gail, please...sit down for just a minute." He pointed to the chair opposite him.

Against my better judgment, I sat down because I didn't know what he would do if I did not do as he asked. "What, what can you possibly say to me, Stewart?"

"I'm sorry. I'm so sorry. Gail, I don't know what happened to me, but I want you to know that sometimes a dark cloud comes over me, and I don't know where I am. I think I am back in Vietnam. I hear the sounds, smell the smells, and see the enemy. As far as I know, I thought you were Viet Cong that night. You were the enemy, and I had to kill you."

"Then why didn't you? I asked.

"I don't know. I don't remember. All I know is that a dark cloud comes over me. It has happened to me before. I should have never been around you and the kids."

"Okay, I heard you, I said, getting up." "I can't talk about this, Stewart." "I can't see you." "Please don't come here again." By now, my whole body was visibly shaking. I thought I was going to die.

"Ok, he said, I won't. Good by, Gail." He walked out. I went in the bathroom and took deep breaths until I could stop the shakes.

My other remedy for all of life's tribulations and jubilations became drinking and taking drugs. By now, I was spiraling out of control and for the first time in my life, I began to fear that I could not take care of my children. The more I tried to figure out what to do, the more the drugs, alcohol, and mental stress of the trauma from Stewart began to take its toll. I became more and more irresponsible, trying to escape the sorrow and fear growing like a monster inside me. I went to work every night feeling guilty about leaving the boys upstairs by themselves. I tried to reason that I was right downstairs, but I knew in my heart that they were not being watched closely enough. I was becoming frantic about the welfare of my children, but I could not stop partying and my boss would not give me the day shift that he had promised when he hired me.

186

My boys walked to school, began complaining that some big boys would meet them in the woods, and beat them up. One day after school, my friend, Sam, met these boys in the woods, and I do not know what happened except that the bullying stopped. However, the boys still hated the school, and I was constantly worried about how my lifestyle was affecting them. By now, there were many friends in and out of my apartment. They were not dangerous people, but they were alcoholics and drug addicts like me, and I was always looking over my shoulder, waiting for Stewart to come blasting through the door with his sawed off shotgun.

I did not have long to wait. One day, I looked up and there he was again strolling into the Swinging Tiger while I was working. This time he was drunk.

I walked over to his table to get his order. He said, "I don't want anything to drink. I just got back from Canada where I killed a man. My gun is in the car."

I had heard him talk like that a couple of times.. I ignored it. "Stewart, why are you coming here?"

"Why, to see you, aren't you glad to see me?" he slurred.

"No, I'm not. Please stop coming in here." I was shaking, always shaking when he was near, frantic and nervous.

"Gail, I go wherever I want, but okay, I'm leaving now, just stopped in to tell you to watch your back. I'll be back." With that, he got up and walked to the door, turned around, glared at me, and walked out.

My whole body went limp, and I had to sit down. Luckily, the day bartender was there and covered for me for a half hour while I went upstairs and forced myself to breathe. Again, I asked my boss if he would give me the day shift. He said, "No, I like you on nights. It's good for business."

"But you promised me when you hired me that I could have the day shift in a couple of weeks. I have the kids."

"I know, but I need you on nights." I knew that was it. He walked away and if I pushed any harder, he would fire me. I was furious and every day I got angrier.

That winter, Sam, my new boyfriend, and a young couple with a baby were making plans to move to southern California. Sam had lived out there and told me it was beautiful. Every since I saw an Elvis movie that was set in California, I had wanted to see it. He told me the weather was always warm and you didn't need heat or winter clothes. That caught my attention because I was always struggling to pay heating bills that were more than my rent. I was constantly juggling bills because my income was less than my bills. I thought, I could support us out there and Stewart would never find me. I knew after the last encounter that I was never going to be free of him, and that one of these times when he was drunk or insane, he would kill me.

That March, I drove to Long Lake and had a long talk with my mother. I told her about Stewart following me. I told her about my California plan. I asked Mom if she and Dad would keep Ricky and Monti until they got out of school in June when I would send for them. My mother said, "Gail, I know you think you are fine, but you are not. You are not emotionally over what Stewart did to you. I think you should go to California, get away, get a good job, and don't let anyone but us know where you are. She told me that they would keep the boys. Mom was also worried about my safety, the boys' safety, and my emotional state. I knew at that time that I could no longer care for my boys, as they needed to be. That thought continued haunting me. My solution was to go back home and drink more so I could not feel the fear and the shame.

The next Friday night, I went to work, got drunk, called my boss, and told him his bartender was drunk. I knew he would fire me. I did not know he would evict me. He did both. He told me I had to be out by Sunday. That night when Sheryl came home, I told her she had to go back to Long Lake because I had

188

lost the apartment. She knew about my conversation with Mom and knew she was going with the kids to Long Lake. She just didn't know it was happening this fast. Sam offered to share his apartment with me until we left for California in two weeks.

Kenneth had picked up the kids on Thursday night to keep them for Easter vacation. I called my mother and told her that Ken would bring the kids to her the following Sunday. Then, I called Kenneth and told him to bring the kids to Long Lake on Sunday to my Mom and Dad's instead of the apartment. I did not tell him I was moving. Before he brought the kids to Long Lake, they stopped at the Swinging Tiger. Someone in the bar told them that I had moved to California; however, I was living three blocks down the road and did not know they had told the boys this story. This man knew I was going to California, but didn't know when, so he thought we had left because he hadn't seen me. He didn't know I had been fired and evicted.

This series of decisions I made affected the lives of my children for years to come. My alcoholism had reached a mental, physical, and spiritual bottom that I never saw coming, and anyone close to me suffered the consequences.

I was nervous about telling the boys I was going to California and that they would be staying with their grandparents for a couple of months, so I procrastinated telling them. I called Mom from Saranac Lake on the Tuesday after Ken had dropped them off, and asked her if she told the boys that I would be going to California. She said, "No, Gail, you need to do that."

I cried, "Mom, I can't. I just can't." I was shaking inside and out and I knew I needed to go down there and tell them. Each day, I put it off, and then suddenly, we were leaving the next day. On that Saturday, Sam said he did not want to wait another week. We took everything out of the apartment, put it in the yard, and sold it, and on Sunday morning, we were on the road. I had not told my children. My mother had to tell them. Today, I know that I had a mental breakdown and it cost me the most important part of me, my children's trust. I never dreamed that on the day they were born, and I looked into their eyes and vowed to protect them, that I would be the monster hurting them. I never dreamed where alcohol would take me. That winter in Saranac Lake is a memory I wish I could erase. It is by far the most demoralizing incomprehensible time in my life, but it happened, and I will never forget it and that is my penance for the enormous injury I laid upon my two sons.

CHAPTER 43

CALIFORNIA HERE I COME

I left for California with a young couple and a newborn baby in one car, while Sam, Denise, and I were in my car. We had no idea where to go in California. Previously, Sam was stationed at Camp Pendleton Marine Corp base in Oceanside, CA, so we decided to go there.

In Texas, my car starter stopped working, Sam and I got into a fight, so he jumped into the other car and they left Denise and me at a rest stop with a broken car and no money. We had pooled our money and given most of it to Sam because he was driving, pumping the gas, and had the pot. Denise started crying, and I started looking for help. I rarely let things deter me when I set my mind on something, and it was set on California.

"Denise, I said, come on, we are waitresses. We can get jobs in the next town and get enough money to go on."

"But how are we even going to get to the next town. The car doesn't work," she cried.

"We're going to ask somebody for a push and then we will only stop where we can park it on a hill. Hey, there is a truck coming in. I'm going to ask the driver to give us a push."

"Are you crazy? He could be a rapist or some other weirdo," Denise replied.

"Well, what are we going to do, sit here all day?"

Her answer was, "Maybe Sam will come back?"

I didn't want to hear anything about him, much less give him the satisfaction of coming back to help us. "You know what Denise, I'll be damned if I'll let that jerk stop me. He doesn't want to be with me, fine, let him ride with them to California. I'll take my chances with a truck driver." I opened the door, walked over to the blue truck, and started yelling, "Hey, mister, mister!"

I could see him through the window—black hair, beard, about fifty years old. He didn't look like an axe murderer, I thought, but we were in the middle of Texas, for God's sake, and there was not another vehicle in the lot. I plunged ahead anyway, walked up to the driver's window, and began jumping up, waving my arms and yelling.

Finally, he rolled down the window. "What's the problem?" he asked.

"Hi, I'm Gail. My girlfriend and I are stranded here in a car with a broken starter. Can you give us a push, so I can pop the clutch?" He followed my glance back to the car. Denise was leaning against the car, face stark white, still crying.

"Sure, I'll help you girls. I stopped to get some coffee and use the rest room. Just give me a few minutes." He got out and headed into the building. I ran back, told Denise, and we waited until he came out.

He came out coffee in hand, walked over, and put his hand out. "My name is Robert.

"This is Denise, thanks for helping."

"Hi Denise, no problem. Where are you going?"

"California," I replied.

"You're going all the way to California with a broken starter?"

"Yes, we'll just keep parking on hills from now on. Listen, Robert, a friend who was with us left us here and took off with all of our money. He got in the car with another couple who came with us."

"Some friend," he said. "Listen, I'm going to Las Vegas." "What city are you headed for?"

"Oceanside," Denise said coming out of her silence.

"Good, Oceanside is about five hours straight out of Vegas. " Follow me and I will keep an eye on you the whole way to Vegas. You stay with me. Now, girls do you know the route out of Vegas to Oceanside?"

192

I showed him our map and he drew us a faster route, turned and walked back toward his truck. "Thank you, I yelled, you are an angel!"

"No, I'm a dad," he replied as I watched him step up into the cab of his truck.

"He's going to help us. See I told you." I announced as I jumped in the car.

"He is a nice man," Denise conceded adding, "but he could have…"

"But he didn't," I interrupted. God, I thought, if she does not stop whining, I'm going to leave her at the next rest stop. We followed him all the way to Las Vegas, at some point, passing Sam, Laurie, and Dave who were parked on the side of the road. I honked the horn and waved as we flew by. Denise droned on about how she wanted to go with them. I ignored her and drove on. I was mad, and I was going to Oceanside no matter what anyone said or did. To hell with all of them, I thought, I'll dump them all when I get there. I had no fear. I knew that if I could work, I could eat and find a place to live.

In Las Vegas, that wonderful man waved us off, and we were on our own flying along the open highway, singing "Hotel California" with the radio, watching the gray Chevrolet in my rear view mirror. I put my blinker on just before the California border. Dave put his blinker on and we pulled over on the side of the road. Sam exited the gray car, sauntered over beer in hand, and apologized to us. I accepted. Denise got into the gray car, and we drove over the border, stopped the cars, got out, and kissed the earth. We were in California! I was ecstatic except for the deep prick in my heart at the thought of my boys. This dark moment was washed away by my scream, "California, here I am!"

There were many painful moments to come. Sam became violent, addicted heavily to drugs, and there were terrifying times of learning about living in a city. One day, I was hitchhiking to work and a man in a van picked me up. He said, "Do you want to have a beer?"

"Sure, I'll have a beer," I flirted back. He drove to a field. I said, "Where are you taking me?"

"Oh just down this road a ways."

"But I don't want to go down here. Stop right now and let me out." By now, we were well away from the city out in the middle of nowhere. He said nothing and continued to drive.

"Please, I changed my mind. I want to get out," I pleaded.

"Okay, he stopped the van, we'll get out then." I got out trembling with fear. He was right behind me with two beers in his hand. He handed me one, took a long drink, and then began to put his arm around me.

I pulled away, "No, I don't want to do that." "I don't even know you." He tried again more forcefully, and I pushed him away. "No, you asked me to come have a beer with you, not sex."

He looked at me and said, "You know I could rape you right now and there would be nothing you could do about it." "You came willingly into my truck." I held my breath and began scanning the place to find a rock or anything I might use as a weapon. "But you are lucky this time little girl, because I'm not going to rape you." "I'm taking you back." "Don't do this again." He took me back and I thanked him. I was blessed and didn't know it. I had angels all along the trail, but could not see them. I learned a little from each one but not enough, nowhere near enough.

I became a master escape artist using alcohol, men, and drugs. They all took me away from those dark nights when the enemy roamed the rooms and ruled over me. One great escape was Denial. By the time I got to California, I simply erased my second marriage from my brain. I had escaped. I was happy with new places, new jobs, new people, new bars, and my children arriving soon.

In May, my happiness changed to anger when Kenneth filed a custody suit and because the courts were backed up, my court date was not scheduled until June of the next year. To make matters worse, my car was history, I had no money for a plane ticket, and I was trying to adjust from small town living to city living. The court granted my parents temporary custody of Ricky and Monti, and I tackled jobs in order to save money for the tickets to go to New York and get my kids. Each day brought more fury at Kenneth who I blamed for taking my children from me. Stewart no longer existed and I perceived myself as a victim of these violent, crazy men including the new crazy one I was trying to keep out of jail and the mental hospital..

Within three weeks of arriving in California, I had two jobs--a waitress job at the Oceanside Bowling alley and a job selling ads at the local newspaper. We slept in my broken car, motel rooms, and then a friend's apartment with no furniture. I slept on the floor. Finally I had enough money to rent an apartment, sharing it with Sam. He had all the criteria for a mate for me. He was jealous, angry, obsessive, a drunk, and an addict. We did acid, smoked pot, drank, and listened to *Queen* blasting in our ears until the sun came up. I wrote to my boys, called them, cried over them, ached for them, and continued to live a lie. I clung to a wishing well Ricky had made me, and my photograph album. I was constantly looking through their baby pictures.. I had written poems for them on their birth dates, at six months old, one year old, and so on. Sam was always mad at me for spending so much time looking at the pictures. Several times he came over and shut the book while I was looking at it, yelling about how I spent more time looking in that book than with him. One day, I came home from work, went to the shelf where I kept the book, and it was gone. I searched frantically everywhere. I even went out to the dumpster and sifted through the contents. I

195

screamed at Sam, "How could you? That was my life! That is all I have of my boys!" He repeatedly denied it, but I knew he did it. That act sealed his fate with me and drove me into enormous pain and sorrow. All my baby pictures, toddler pictures, gone; it was as if my whole world disappeared. All I wanted to do was sleep. I finally was able to buy a bed, and now I had to force myself out of it to go to work.

In addition, during this time, Sam became increasingly physically violent and distant. One night I came home from work early and caught him with the woman who lived next door. I cried, stayed in bed all day until work, and watched him leave every night to stay with the new girlfriend. Each day, I dragged myself out of bed just in time to go to work at the bowling alley at 5:00 PM. Soon, I began looking in the newspaper for a new place. I found one, and one day right after Sam left to go to the girlfriend's, I dashed into the bedroom, threw everything I could fit into a box, and walked out the door never to return, never to give Sam my new address or telephone number. Two nights later, he showed up at the bowling alley drunk. Since I had already warned the bouncer (who was from Samoa and as big as an elephant) about Sam, he ran interference for me, forcing this shouting crazy man to leave the building. Sam came back to the bowling alley three times, threatened me, and then he settled down with the new girlfriend who now paid his rent and ducked his fists.

I moved to a wonderful red wood house on a dead end street just outside of Oceanside. It had a large yard where I immediately imagined the boys and me playing baseball. Inside, the walls were knotty pine, one wall housing a gigantic rock fireplace. It looked like a huge ski lodge, and I loved it immediately because it reminded me of home. It was also old, and abandoned. The landlord agreed to keep the rent low if I did not bother him with repairs, etc., so I learned how to be a plumber, an electrician, and many other handywoman jobs while

196

living in that house poor as beggar. When I first moved into the house, I shared it with a roommate; however, he eventually moved, and it became mine.

Sam came back into my life a couple of times after that, but only as a fellow Adirondacker whom I felt obligated to help. He was at times like a child and could barely function, and I helped get him off Thorazine and out of the mental hospital. He did come and live with me a few years later, as I was the only person who would take care of him; however, that ended abruptly when I came home from work one day and discovered that he had dismantled all the lamps in the house. He said they were broken and he was fixing them. With a police officer boyfriend's help, I had the Marshall come and take him to the hospital. I will never forget the sad look on his face as they took him away in the police car. My heart hurt for him, but I could not safely take care of him.

It was about this time that Mike Tracy almost came back in my life. We had never really lost touch with each other. Sometimes I called him in the middle of the night drunk and lonesome, and sometimes he called me. He was mad that I had gone to California, but I reminded him that he was living with another woman and could be mad all he wanted because I didn't care. The phone calls always ended with both of professing our love for one another. By this time I was a blackout drinker-- when I drank I did not remember saying or doing things sometimes for hours, or sometimes the whole night. I soon found out that blackouts were not good for making life-changing decisions.

One morning around six o'clock, after an all nighter, the telephone rang. My head was pounded, my throat felt like dried canvas, and I yelled at the phone for disturbing my two-hour sleep.

"Hello," I mumbled.

"Gail?"

"Yes, who is this?"

"It's Mike."

"Mike who?"

"What to hell do you mean, Mike who?" "It's me, Mike Tracy and I'm on my way."

"Oh, Mike, Hi, where are you going?"

"What do you mean where am I going? I'm coming out there."

With that, I sat straight up in bed. "You're what?"

He said, "I've sold everything and the truck is packed and I'm on my way."

My swollen brain tried to piece together what he was saying. I began thinking, oh my God. I don't want him out here. I had been flirting and going out and being free. I was having fun. I was single, living in southern California where there were three men to every woman. I loved the attention and the freedom.

"Why did you do that, Mike?"

"Because you told me to."

"I did not."

"You did, too!" he shouted back.

"When did we talk about this?"

"Are you nuts? I called you twice and both times, you asked me to come to California. The first time was a few weeks ago. You said you loved me and missed me."

"I did?"

"For God's sake, Gail, you don't remember?"

I did not, but I did not want him to know that, so I said, "Oh, yes, now I remember. I don't know why I said that. I do love you, Mike, but I am not ready to live with you."

"Well, isn't that just great. I quit my job for you."

"I'm sorry," I said meekly.

"You should be sorry. Don't ever call me again, Gail!" he shouted and slammed the phone down hard. I felt bad for

198

about two seconds, but mostly I felt relieved because I was not interested in having him come out and spoil my fun. By now, I was hiking all through the high desert with friends, had applied for a job with the local police department with the help of a police officer who flirted with me every morning at the bowling alley. I knew Mike was not lying. I must have talked to him when I was drunk. We were finally done and I vowed that I would never go there again.

CHAPTER 44

KIDNAPPING CUSTODY

I continued to work and drink. Slowly, the drug use began to wane. I was obsessed with getting my children back. During this time, I got a third job. I met a nice man, Bob, who had a plane and took me flying. Bob knew I needed money, and that I had an accounting degree, so with his influence, I landed a part-time job at the local airport.

Our friendship grew and one day I told Bob about my boys. I cried and lamented to him how much I missed them and how I could not remove them from New York State. By now, I was working around the clock trying to save money for plane tickets and court. One day while flying with my friend, I said, "I wish we could just keep going to New York, swoop down, get my boys, and fly away."

He said, "I'll fly you to New York."

"What, I was kidding," I said. Then, the idea began floating in my brain until by the time we touched ground, I had a plan to fly to New York, kidnap my children, and live in Mexico in peace. To describe the relationship I had with this man who was now taxiing along the runway would be a father daughter relationship. He was married; financially solvent, helped the underdog, and drank too much alcohol.

Soon, the plan was real, and I was going to steal my children. I called my mother, who immediately told me not to do it. I told her that I would come in the night and get them and she could just say she did not hear me, so she would not get in trouble.

"Gail, you are not doing that," was her reply.

"But this is the only way," I pleaded.

"No, it is not." They would arrest you for kidnapping, you would go to jail, and how would that help those boys? They are in school and they are happy. Their cousins are next door and they are together all the time. You just keep working and come here for the court date."

One thing I knew more than anything about my mother is that she was wise. Even though my emotions and my fears were powerful forces pushing me to get what I wanted, I listened and obeyed my mother. "Ok," I said sobbing, tears flowing freely now. I had gone from exhilaration over a plan to be with my children to a deep dark hole. I will never get them back, I thought.

Then I heard her voice soothing me, "Gail, you will get them. You just have to have patience. They love you and you were a good mother. I am sure the judge will give them to you." I began to feel a ray of hope, and slowly the reality of consequences of my plan began to sink in.

"I'm sorry. You're right, Mom. All I can do is wait for court. Thank you so much for caring for them." Then I told the children that Mom was better, and she was doing everything she could to get them back and we would be together again soon. In the meantime, we wrote letters, talked to each other on the telephone, and I continued to stabilize emotionally, work and save money.

I enjoyed my part time job at the air school and planned to take flight lessons. Bob had already taught me the instrument panel, and Tom, one of the partners was teaching me the basics. One morning I arrived at work, unlocked the door, and was dumbstruck at what I saw. Terry, one of the partners, sat at the desk with his head in his hands. File drawers were wide open, and papers were scattered across the floor and the desks. "Terry, what, what happened here, were we robbed?"

Terry looked up. His face was red. His long strawberry blond hair hung loosely around his face. His sky-blue eyes were now dull. I could tell he had been crying. "Gail, it was Tom."

"What?" I couldn't grasp what he was saying. "What was Tom? Is he okay? Where is he?"

"He's gone."

"Gone? Gone where?" I just couldn't grasp what he was saying.

"I wish I knew. He was the robber, Gail. He took all the money out of the accounts and flew off in the Queen Air. I don't know what I'm going to do."

I turned and looked out the glass door. Sure enough, the beautiful white airplane was gone. Finally, it hit home. Oh my God, he cleaned out Terry. How could he do that? I rushed over to Terry. He stood up, and I held him while he sobbed, saying he didn't know what he would do now. All his money was in the business. "We need to call the police, Terry. Did you call them?"

"Yes, they are on their way." A few minutes later a detective came and interviewed both of us. I went to the books and turned them over to the detective. We discovered that Tom was keeping a separate set of books all along. Mine were actually fakes. He had hired me to keep fake books and I didn't have a clue. Apparently, Tom was a crook. I stayed and helped Terry out as much as I could with salvaging what he could out of the business. He could no longer pay me, so I soon left. I expected a court subpoena when they caught Tom but never received one, so maybe he flew off to some foreign country, never to be heard from again. Bob and I slowly stopped seeing each other when he began hinting at turning our friendship into more than friendship.

Did I accept what my mother told me? Yes. Did I drop the frantic goal to have my boys? No. Once my mind locked onto something, not much can stop it. The only power I know that can stop it is God and God wasn't stopping my brain or my fingers when I dialed Kenneth's number and tried to reason with him again for what seemed like the millionth time. This time the discussion centered on him telling me there was an investigator in Oceanside hired by the court to check up on me.

To that, I said, "Kenneth, I work for the police department and the newspaper. My friends are all police officers. I live in a nice house in a nice neighborhood with a big yard for the kids. I have always been a good mother. I stayed home night after night with them from the time they were babies while you were out in the bars. You beat me and the priests at church know it, and the Saranac Lake police have records of my calls. You never took care of those boys by yourself, never changed a diaper, fed them a bottle, or read them stories. You were gone for two years and Monti barely knows you. I have never tried to get child support from you, even when you disappeared without a word. Kenneth, I know you love those boys, but I am their mother, and they need me. Please, drop this custody case. Do you really want the responsibility of caring for them if you should win custody? Do you really want to take them away from me?"

His answer was, "No, Gail, I never wanted to take them away from you. I know they love you and you love them. I know you are closer to them than I am, and I know I don't know how to take care of them."

"Then why are you trying to take my babies?" I began crying. I could not talk about them without crying.

"Well, Mom…"

I cut in, "Mom? Irene is pushing you isn't she? Is she going to take care of them?"

"Well, no she can't." His mother was now elderly and partially disabled.

"So, you will be cooking their breakfast, shopping for their food, clothes, and everything else they need, and you will be cooking their dinner, taking them to their games, going to report card night and taking care of them when they are sick, and taking them to the dentist?" I went on and on in this vein for several minutes. "Kenneth, be realistic and think about what is best for our boys. Can you really take care of them?"

"To be honest, Gail, it scares me to death. I do not think I can, and I feel so guilty taking them away from you."

"Then let me have them. Let them be with their mother." It was then that I heard the most glorious words in the entire world spoken to me at that time.

"Okay, Gail, I'll drop the custody suit."

I held my breath. I was speechless, and my brain could not believe what my ears had heard. "Really?" is all I could blurt out, expecting him to say some cruel thing like are you crazy. I'm just kidding.

"Really." His voice was low. I knew he loved his children but his mother was a powerful force in his life. "The boys need to be with you. You have always been a good mother. I hated you for leaving me, and I know you had to because of the things I did, but I always loved the way you loved our boys. I was worried about them, but I know they need to be with you. I will go to the lawyer and tell him to stop the suit."

I could not believe this was the same man who had screamed through the phone lines at me, accused me of all kinds of things he had done, not me, and called me every foul name he could think of. I still did not believe he was doing it. I could not let myself have hope. Hope was not an option for me. It hurt, but the next day he called and told me he signed the papers. That time, I believed him. By the end of the week, I had the letter from the court saying the suit was dropped and the boys could be taken out of the state. I felt like I was floating. I smiled constantly and called everyone to tell them my children were coming. My three jobs had paid off, and I had the money for their airline tickets. I immediately arranged to fly Ricky and

Monti out to California to a new life where we would be together and live happily ever after.

CHAPTER 45

JUNE, 1979, COMING HOME

I will never forget seeing them come through the door at the San Diego airport, Ricky with his big blue eyes and little Monti with a grin as a big as a crescent moon, running toward me and wrapping my arms around them. My God, the smell, the smell of them was overwhelming to me. To touch them, feel their hair, feel their little bodies against mine. It was heaven on earth, and we all cried. Time stopped, and I could revel in the essence of their presence. Thank you, God, I whispered as I let go, stood back and looked at these beautiful little boys now a head taller. There was no fear in their faces as I had expected. I am sure there was fear but it was overshadowed by bright jumping eyes and smiling faces.

Arriving home, they ran through the house finding their rooms and within thirty minutes, we were in the backyard playing baseball. I already had them enrolled in school, and by the end of that year, Ricky received a ribbon for "Most Outstanding student." I was so proud as I watched him shyly walk up and get his ribbon. They were excellent athletes, so I enrolled them in all of the sports, came to their games, cheered too loudly they said, yet every time they went out to play, their heads turned, searching for my face in the bleachers. I never missed a game and even ended up coaching part of a season. I played softball on the Oceanside Police women's team, and on weekends, we camped at Big Bear, Yosemite, or one of the numerous canyons throughout California. We would all hike, swim in the cold rivers and creeks, cook hotdogs and marshmallows over the campfire, and play guitar and sing. My friend, Cindy, and I drank beer and smoked pot, and the boys, who were now ten and eleven, whooped and raced through the

207

campsite, drinking soda and playing with whatever friend they brought with them, usually Darren and William. At this time, I was a California working hippy mom, cheering for legalization of marijuana because I rationalized that it was a harmless plant like tobacco and should not be banned. That is how my brain could twist perception to justify whatever I wanted to do.

Our home became the teenage hang out. I was a young Mom, smoked pot, loved kids, and played sports, so I suppose I was cool to these boys. Darren became a fixture at our house and lived with us for two years. William lived with us during the summer and went home in the winter for school. Darren's parents were bizarre people, changing religions as often as most people change cars, dragging him off to whatever church they were attending now, from Jehovah Witness to Buddhism to a motorcycle club where his father drove a Harley. Darren preferred our insanity to his own, so he stayed with us. Williams's parents drank alcohol and did drugs, apparently more than I did, so William escaped to our house whenever he could. We were a family, and though I never had much money, I thought all was well, as I popped another Budweiser and rolled another joint.

CHAPTER 46

RULES AND RUNAWAYS

Drinking took me down to places I never thought I would go. Alcohol became my boss, my husband, and my first love. Though I always knew I could never love anyone more than my children, I was wrong. I loved alcohol. I loved the way it took the fear away, it made the cold in my bones thaw; and it made the world turn right again, in my mind.

In the summer of 1980, I was coming home from work determined I would not drink today. By now, I was making promises to my children that I would not drink or that I would only drink on weekends. One early evening, as usual, I swore I would not drink after work, and as usual, my car as if by remote control turned into the 7-11 parking lot. I exited out of the car, and took a step toward the brightly lit building, when, suddenly, a thought hit me like a giant thunderbolt, I cannot stop drinking. It frightened me for a moment. Immediately, I shoved this thought deep into the recesses of my mind and continued walking into the store to get beer.

When the boys confronted me about my promise, I argued that at least I was home with them. I skipped over the nights that I called home at five o'clock saying I would be right home after a couple of drinks, but came rolling in one more time at 2:00 AM. I would wake up the next morning, watch those children go out the door to school, and feel like the lowest snail on earth and wonder why, why I continued to do this. There were loud parties at the red house with bands and the police, whom I knew, rolling in and telling me to shut it down, but I was home with my kids; therefore, not guilty.

I had to have roommates in order to pay the bills. At this time, I was making $3.80 per hour at the police station and every two weeks I ran out of money before the next paycheck. We ate macaroni and tomatoes and peanut butter sandwiches quite frequently. When I rented the extra bedroom and the garage, it was as if we were rich. At this time, my life was chaotic; however, I did have a few rules.

Number one rule: The boys could not drink alcohol, though I had no marijuana rule.

Number two rule: The children could not smoke cigarettes (I smoked).

Number three rule: No selling drugs from my house.

I issued these rules to my kids and roommates, but one roommate broke number three. He was a big man with long black hair tied in a ponytail. He did not drink much, but he smoked pot, which was fine with me. He was very quiet and unassuming and agreed to all of the rules. Three months later, I found out Ben was selling pot out in front of my house. Little did I know that this action was the least of my problems with this man.

In August 1980, I started a new job in Carlsbad as an office manager for a marriage and family counseling firm. I had to be there at 7:00 AM to open up. Consequently, some nights I was in bed and asleep by 8:00 or 9:00 PM. The boys would stay up later. This was one of those nights. I said good night to them and went to sleep. At around 6:00 AM the telephone rang. I thought it was the alarm. By the second ring, I realized it was the telephone, so I picked it up and said a groggy, "Hello"

"Hello, Gail, this is Mike."

"Mike?"

"Yes, your brother, Mike."

"Oh, hi, wow, why are you calling so early? Are you ok?"

"Yes, I am Gail, but your kids aren't."

"What?" I sat up on the bed, now very alert.

"Gail, I have your kids."

"What are you talking about; my kids are asleep in their bedroom?" My thoughts went back to last night. They were both sitting on the couch watching the game when I hugged them good night and went to bed.

"No, they aren't, Gail. They are here. Go look, go look right now."

"Ok," I said, completely bewildered, knowing they were in their bedrooms. I jumped off the bed and raced into their bedroom expecting to see them there, thinking my brother must be drunk even though he didn't sound it. I opened their door, and saw Monti sleeping under his covers. I breathed a sigh of relief wondering if Mike had gone off the deep end, as I walked in and pulled Monti's blanket down. I froze when I saw the pillows lined up under the blanket. I ran to Ricky's bed and found the same thing. I stared in disbelief. It felt like all the blood drained out of my body. I couldn't believe it. I ran through the house looking in rooms and calling their names. Then, I saw a piece of paper on Ricky's bed. I picked it up. It said, "Mom, I'm sorry. We love you." I stood there, riveted to the floor in shock. Then I remembered my brother. I ran back to telephone.

"Why, why are they in Virginia? How did they get there?" I stammered by now crying loud and long wounded to the soul at the second loss of my children.

"I sent them a plane ticket and your roommate took them to the airport," he explained.

"You, you sent them an airline ticket?" "Yes, they told me that it wasn't safe there and that you were abusing them."

"And you sent them a ticket without even calling me, without even discussing this with me?" I asked incredulously.

"Yes, I was worried about them."

"Mike, how could you take my babies away from me? Were you drunk when you sent them the tickets?"

"No."

"Don't you know, they probably just called to tell you stuff and that some of it may be exaggerated because they are twelve and thirteen years old?"

"Well, I believed them," he said. "They said you swung them around and let them go and they hurt themselves."

I wracked my brain, "swung them around?" I could not comprehend what he was saying or why they would say that. Then I remembered that quite often we played a game where they would bet that they were now big enough to wrestle me to the floor. Last week, we had wrestled and I won. During that wrestle, I did spin them around, but I did not let them fly. They were mad, but they were not hurt. I explained this to Mike. "I did wrestle with them, but it was in fun." They were good-sized boys now, and it never occurred to me that they would resort to such measures.

"Well, I don't know. Maybe you played too hard. They said they got hurt."

I began to feel hot anger seething through me like a snake. "Mike, you will not keep my kids from me! I will get them back," I spat as I hung up the telephone. I called in sick to work and immediately called all the legal places I could think of. For hours, I sat on that telephone, dialing numbers, determined to keep calling until somebody helped me. Finally, the next afternoon, I was speaking to the California district attorney. He assured me that no one could take my children and that my recourse was to charge my brother with kidnapping. I told him, I did not want to do this, but I would as a last resort. He contacted the district attorney in Virginia who called the government office where Mike worked. They informed him that he would be charged with kidnapping if he kept my children. I loved my brother with all my heart, but I loved my children more. They needed me; I knew it and they knew it. They had found a way to get back at me for leaving them. When Mike understood the ramifications of a felony kidnapping charge, he immediately

212

took them to their stepfather, Mike Tracy, who lived in Winchester, VA, sixty miles away. Mike Tracy agreed to pay for half of their bus ticket back to California. I paid for the other half of the ticket.

They had a long, hot ride back to California, looking sheepish and scared when they got off the bus. I was just happy to have them home. As I hugged them and looked in their eyes, I knew part of this escapade was to show me what it felt like to wake up and find out the person you love the most is gone. My roommate and my brother were pawns in their scheme. Later, they told me they were mad when they called Uncle Mike, and they never believed he would purchase airline tickets. When they found out he bought them the tickets, they felt like they had to go. They were two little boys trying to make sense of an upside down world. My brother was trying to do what he thought was best for his nephews. My roommate, Ben, escaped death by finding a new place to live.

CHAPTER 47

THE LEGACY OF STEWART

On a balmy March day at 2:40 PM, Stewart died of Cirrhosis of the Liver. I received a telegram, asking me to sign for the cremation. I was angry because that little piece of paper forced me to acknowledge that I was married to this man. I still did not acknowledge this marriage in my life in California. I could not think about what happened that night in Cedarland Park, because it brought on tremors, sweating, nightmares, and overwhelming fear. I remember one time someone from back home told me he was in Colorado. I thought he had found out where I was and was coming for me. It was terrifying, but, now, he would never find me. I did not grasp the concept that his death could be a foreshadowing of what could happen to me, because I reasoned that I did not hide alcohol in the woods and get up every two hours to have a drink, so I was not an alcoholic. When I signed my name on the permission form, I felt a twinge of sadness, but by now, my own drinking had taken me to an unforgiving place that allowed no clemency for him, or any other man. Now, I stayed home, drank and existed in no man's land—could not stay sober, could not get drunk. I worked, attended my boy's ballgames, and teacher's conferences, suffered horrendous nightmares, and drank every night.

In August, my landlord sent me a letter telling me we had to move because his daughter was moving back to California and would move into the red house. I was frantic. I knew I could not find another house in a decent neighborhood that we could afford. This house was in complete ill repair. I fixed toilets with shoelaces, and prayed that the old wiring would hold out while we were there and did not bother the landlord with anything. In turn, he kept the rent low.

One day, while eating lunch with my boss, George, he asked me why I was not married. For some reason, maybe because he was a counselor or just a nice man, I told him the truth about my second marriage. He said, "Gail, I was a drug and alcohol counselor in the Navy before I opened this business."

"Oh," I said, stiffening up, thinking he was going to ask me about my drinking. I had actually made a vow to quit that Halloween. It was December and I was not drinking. I was miserable, still smoked pot, but I had not had a drink since October 31.

George continued, "Since your husband was a lifer, I assume you are getting benefits, right."

"No."

"No; why not?"

"I don't know what you mean?"

"Didn't the Navy send you information?"

"Now I remembered many months ago, receiving a blue book in the mail. I refused to look at it. Well, maybe, I think they sent me a blue book a long time ago."

"Yes, that's it. Did you read it?"

"No." I took a breath and began to tell him the whole story. It was the first time I had told anyone. I could not finish because of the tremors, but he heard enough to tell me that I needed to contact the Navy. I repeated telling him that I could not do that because it was too painful and too frightening. I told him I could not talk anymore, so he dropped it. That night, I looked at the blue cover of the Navy pamphlet they had sent me, but I did not open it. That night the nightmare was horrific with my head being severed and rolled down a hill into a dark hole.

A week later, George called me into his office and proposed that I go with him to the Camp Pendleton military base and get the benefit paperwork done. He told me he had contacted a woman he knew who did the paperwork, told her my circumstances, and she said she would put aside whatever amount of time it took for me to get through the paperwork. I immediately said, "No." What had happened to me scared deep, and all my bravery, courage, and toughness disintegrated at the thought of telling another soul about my ordeal.

Then he said the magic words, "Gail, if you won't do it for you, do it for the children. At least get the school benefits. How are you going to pay for college for them? This could help." Apparently, your husband wanted this for them.

"Really," I said, not believing anything he said, but the words "For your children," trumped fear, so I reluctantly agreed to do it if he went with me. He assured me we would stop when I needed to, whether it took two or three days to fill out the paperwork. It took two days.

I met George at the office at 8:00 AM and he drove me to the Camp Pendleton office. I was petrified and started shaking before even getting through the first door. George put his arm around my shoulders and continued to encourage me to go in. He introduced me to the woman who would ask me the questions. She seemed very kind and told me she had blocked off all morning to help me with this task. Since my hands shook so badly, she filled out the forms for me, and I signed them holding my breath to keep my hand still enough to write a signature. Within one hour, I was shaking so badly, I vomited. That was the end of that session. True to his word, George brought me back the next day and this wonderful woman patiently finished my paperwork.

It was here that I learned that my husband had been hospitalized in the mental ward twice during his time in the Navy, once after receiving a severe head wound in Vietnam. I remembered him showing me the scars, and I remembered hugging him and thanking him for his bravery. The second time was when he severely attacked his first wife and son and put them in the hospital.

Many beautiful people had helped me up to this point in my life; however, I could not see the spirit in them because I could not allow even a slice of goodness into my broken heart. My alcoholic life was filled with catastrophes; blocking all goodness and Godliness.

CHAPTER 48

JACK AND JILL WENT UP THE HILL
TO FETCH A PAIL OF WATER
JACK FELL DOWN AND BROKE HIS CROWN
AND JILL CAME TUMBLING AFTER.

Stewart's death affected me for about three months. I did not drink, but I was angry with everyone else who drank. I was miserable, holed up in the house, listening to the neighbors partying, yelling at God, but not drinking.

In January of 1981, I took the boys to Big Bear, CA skiing. Friday night they went skiing, and I stayed in the lodge with Cindy. She drank beer, and I drank coke. By Saturday afternoon, I had figured out a way to have a beer. I simply would only drink when I came to Big Bear. This was a viable solution until Sunday when we drove out of Big Bear, and I still had a beer in my hand, so I changed the rules to, I would not drink in Oceanside. I was still drinking when we arrived in Oceanside, so the rules changed again to only drinking on weekends.

By the end of January, I was drinking even more than before I quit on Halloween. I drank every night after work and every weekend; however, now, I only drank at home so I could be with the kids. In reality, that was a half-truth. The other reasons for home isolation were the cost of my increasingly high tolerance to alcohol and my embarrassing black outs. For a while, I adapted to this memory loss by pretending to recall talking to people and going to places; however, I became so ashamed of things people told me I did and said, that I began to stay at home and drink. The thought that a simpler solution would be to put the drink down never consciously occurred to me.

Another looming predicament was that we had to move out of the house by May 15, and we had no place to go. I had no credit, and my salary was too small to pay for any two-bedroom apartment or house I found in the paper. I did not have the deposit they required. I was so scared, that I began to get on my knees at night and pray to God. I went to the temple across the street, sat on the stone bench, and begged God to help me.

I was working at the office in the daytime and selling Kirby vacuum cleaners at night. I had to keep two jobs just to pay living expenses and buy my cases of rotgut beer to survive on. My girlfriend, Cindy, helped me out with that. She would come over with a case and leave half of it in my refrigerator. I also managed to lure men in, always keeping them at arms length away. They kept me company and bought me beer and pot. Many were just friends, awaiting a change in status to boyfriend. It would never come, because I had built an impenetrable wall that no one could get through.

One day in April, I opened the mailbox and took out a long white envelope addressed to me. It was from the Department of the Navy. I opened it, took out a letter, and saw a thin piece of paper with what looked like a check at the bottom for a few thousand dollars. I stared at it in disbelief. My first thought was that it was a fake check like the ones from Publishers Clearing House. The letter said it was "retroactive." I did not know what that meant. I ran into the house, called my friend, Thomason, and told him briefly, about what I received. I asked him if he would look at the check and tell me if it was real.

"Sure, he answered, come on down." I raced out the door and ran almost the whole mile to the Police Department because my 1962 Volkswagen was broken again. I walked into his office out of breath and handed him the papers. "Thomason, is this real?" "It isn't, is it?"

He took the papers, looked at the check, read the letter, and said, "This is a real check, Gail."

"You mean I can take it to the bank and they will give me money for it?"

"Yes, but…"

"Oh my God, oh my God!" I shouted. I jumped up and down, hugged him, and went flying out the door. I had never seen a check this big before.

"Wait a minute, Gail. What are you going to do with the money? Thomason asked. Do you have a plan?"

"A plan?" I stopped for a moment. You know what; this could not have come at a better time because we have to move. What a coincidence, huh?"

"Right, Gail, a coincidence. I suggest you use some of it for a down payment on a car that runs." For over a year, my Volkswagen was broken more than it ran. Several times, he had to come and take me home or push the car home with his police car. "If you want help picking out a car, let me know." I always called this wonderful man by his last name. He loved me, and he wanted to marry me. I liked him as a friend, used him, and knew deep down that he was the type of man I should love. Loving a man was not option anymore. My walls were impenetrable.

"Wow, I squealed excitedly, I can have a real car. I have to go home now. The kids will be getting home from school, and I can't wait to tell them. Thanks, I'll call you." I hugged him, ran outside, and yelled at the sky, "Thank you, God, thank you!" My mind was racing. Now, we could move into a new place. This would pay first and last months rent and maybe another month. When the boys got home from school, I showed them the check, and we all screamed and jumped around the living room.

In the midst of the excitement, in the recesses of my mind, I remembered Stewart making me sign some papers. After we married, he kept showing me some legal looking papers and telling me I needed to sign them. I kept procrastinating and telling him I would.

One morning he pointed to the table and commanded, "Gail, sit down here at the table." I thought he was going to tell me something bad had happened. I sat down and looked up at him. He reached over, picked up the pen on the table and put it in my hand. "Now, you are going to sign these before you do anything else today." I looked down and saw the pile of papers on the table in front of me. I did not read them, just signed them as he asked. After I signed, he said, "Thank you. Now I feel better."

"Okay, but I'm late for work. Is that it?"

"That's it," he replied, as he sat down in his rocker, coffee in hand and turned on the news. I kissed him quickly, turned to go, and he said, "Gail, you know I love you, don't you?"

I pulled back and looked at his face. "Sure, I know, Stewart, and I love you."

"No, I mean I have always loved you, from the first moment I saw you on the bus. I have loved you through all the years. Did you know that?"

"No, Stewart, I didn't," I replied puzzled but loving him more than ever. "I am sorry, honey, but I have to go now."

"That's okay, I just wanted you to know that." "See you when you get back."

Now, as I walked into the bank, I remembered how important this was to him, and I looked up wondering if he was smiling. Amazingly, this money provided just enough money to relocate and purchase a car. We moved to a middle class neighborhood on El Monty Street in Oceanside. We all loved the house, but problems were brewing just ahead.

My sons started skipping school, and I began a rapid decline into the depths of demoralization. One late morning, after a rough night, I glanced in the mirror, something I rarely did anymore. The woman looking back at me had dull white skin, and dark circles under her red-rimmed eyes. Her brown hair hung in strands down to her thin shoulders. Who is this person, I thought? Where is Gail?

By now, my only friend was Thomason because he was the only person who tolerated me. I was amazed at how he could drink every night, and still get up, and go to work. Many mornings, I was so sick I had to call in and tell a lie because I could not get my head off the pillow, or I was still drunk. George, my boss, was doing most of my work because what was once easy for me, now, was too difficult. My office manager job entailed setting appointments, handling insurance, and balancing the books. I was managing the clients, but I could no longer balance the books. I knew it was only a matter of time before George would have to fire me; however, I could not stop drinking no matter what the circumstances or consequences.

I remember Monti coming home from school one day and saying, "Mom, are you still drunk?" It hurt like the cut of a knife, but it did not stop me. There were still other remarks from the boys. I knew they were embarrassed. I saw them try to hide my beer, and I knew that this woman looking out at me in the mirror with sunken eyes was a mere skeleton of the young girl who ran bravely past the rose bushes and through the woods. That girl was gone and what was in her place was something the world could do without. I thought of suicide, but I would not leave my children again. I still remembered *The Voice* from ten years ago when I tried to kill myself, saying, "No man is worth this." I remember wanting more than anything in the world to stay alive when Stewart tried to kill me. I was a survivor. Suicide by anything other than alcohol was no longer an option.

CHAPTER 49

THE BEGINNING

On June 9, 1981 after drinking all night, I drove to Thomason's house at 5:00 AM. He was asleep. I woke him up and told him I wanted to talk. I poured myself a vodka and ginger ale and was already drinking it when he came stumbling out of the bedroom. Gail, "I just went to bed two hours ago. What do you want?"

"I told you I want to talk," I slurred.

"Okay, talk," he grumbled. He shut his eyes and promptly went to sleep sitting in the chair.

I jumped up, raced out the screen door slamming it hard, and yelled, "I can't talk to you; you're nothing but a drunk!"

I slid onto the seat of my car, drink in hand, and turned the ignition key. Suddenly, I saw a dark tunnel floating right in front of my eyes. At the end of the tunnel, I saw a light. Then, I heard *The Voice* resounding up through the tunnel. It sounded as clear as the crow's caw, "Gail, you are a drunk, you are not a good mother, and your dreams are just dreams. You are going to die if you keep doing what you are doing."

"No!" I screamed. I jammed my foot down on the gas peddle and spun out of the driveway. I cried all the way home. I was not drunk even though I had been drinking for two days straight. I walked through the living room noticing only the brown rug. I looked around me, went into the bathroom, and looked in the mirror. Who was this person? I disgusted me. I had to turn my head to avoid seeing what I had become. My life raced before like a movie film—what I had done, not done. I felt complete demoralization. Guilt seared through me like liquid fire. I slumped down on the couch, wondering whether my children would be better off without me. Laying there unable to sleep or focus, my eyes fell on the yellow telephone book. I stood up, walked over to the book, opened it as if in a trance, looked under alcohol, and dialed the first number. It was 7:30 AM, and a woman answered. For some reason, I was not shocked even though I had no concept of whom I had called. I told her I did not know what was wrong with me or if this was where I should call, but I could not go on with my life as it was.

She said, "I understand. I once felt that way too. You do not have to feel that way again. There is help." She asked me, "Do you think you are an alcoholic?"

"Uh, no, I don't know," I sobbed.

"Are you drinking now?" she asked.

I looked down at the glass on the counter and for some reason did not lie, "Yes," I muttered.

"Do you want to stop drinking?"

"Yes, I think I do." I lied. I did not want to stop drinking because that was not my problem, but something possessed me to tell her I did. I looked down at the amber colored liquid in the glass sitting on the counter. I had not touched that drink since picking up the telephone. She told me to go to a meeting at 8:15 PM at the Oceanside Alano Club. I knew the road since it was on the way to the Camp Pendleton Marine Corp base turnoff. I did not think I was an alcoholic, but I poured out the rest of that drink, put the telephone down, and went to sleep.

That night, I drove to my first meeting. I was shaking, and terrified. I pulled into the parking lot and stared for a while at the cement building, debating whether to go in. I thought about my life, my children, and the tunnel experience the night before. I opened the car door, walked across the seemingly endless parking lot, trudged up the long white steps, and opened the door.

I saw a coffee counter across the room and some old men sitting at little tables playing cards. One of them got up, came over, and asked me if I was looking for the meeting.

226

"Yes," I replied sheepishly. He touched my arm with a gentleness I will never forget, opened a door to the right, and escorted me into a brightly lit room with a big table in the middle where people were sitting and talking. I thanked him, took a chair, and scanned the room seeing mostly more gray-haired men. The man at the head of the table opened the meeting, and then each person starting on the leader's left said their name followed by the phrase, "and I am an alcoholic." I was petrified. I was one of the last people on the right. I did not know what to do. I am not an alcoholic, I thought. What do I say? What do I always do when cornered? I lie. Finally, it was my turn. My voice quivered, but I said, "My name is Gail, and I am an alcoholic." Immediately, my shoulders began to feel weightless, as if about 1000 pounds fell from them.

I remember nothing of the rest of the meeting except at the end they said, "Keep coming back." After that meeting, two women introduced themselves and welcomed me. I do not remember anything they said. I remember their kindness, and I left that meeting with a sliver of hope. I did come back, even though I did not think I was an alcoholic. I could not get my own coffee because I shook so badly, so thank God, they had carafes of coffee on the table and somebody next to me would pour me a cup. I had to drink it with both hands to keep it from spilling. Everything was an ordeal. Another ordeal was calling people. Women gave me their telephone numbers and told me to call them, but physically it was extremely difficult because my short-term memory was barely functioning. I would put the paper down, look at the telephone number, take my eyes away to dial it and forget the number. There was much discussion among the old-timers whether to put me in the hospital. I told them I could not do that because I had no insurance and no money, and two children to feed.

A woman named Phyllis befriended me. She took me to the store and bought me orange juice and honey, drove me to her house and told me to drink it and keep drinking it. That was my detox—orange juice and honey and staying close to this program. In 1981 in southern California, there were few treatment centers. For poor people like me, it was San Diego Detox, the hospital, or these people took care of you. I did not have convulsions and soon graduated from orange juice to ice cream. I came to my first meeting dressed in my one pair of dirty jeans, a worn shirt I loved that said GROG on the front of it and flip-flops. No one laughed. No one told me not to wear that shirt. They knew that might be the only shirt I owned. They were not far off. Clothes were a luxury of rich people, and I had all I could do to keep my boys clothed and fed. Of course, soon I began to feel better and my ego kicked in, telling me how I gorgeous I looked with my stringy vitamin-starved hair, stark white face and sexy skinny body. I was up and running. I remember telling Phyllis how I didn't think I was an alcoholic because I didn't go to jail or steal like some of the others.

She said, "More will be revealed," and walked away smiling. I heard that phrase many times that first year. Sometimes I felt like I had it altogether, and other times I would get in my car, start for work where I had been going for three years, and forget where I was going. I had to quit the job with the marriage and family counselors because I simply could not do it anymore. I knew I could no longer hide the fact that I was not an intelligent person. I had to accept that I was slow or mentally handicap. I got a job in the kitchen at the club making lunch for the noon meeting. It was perfect for me—very simple, few items on the menu, and people with patience of gold for a struggling newcomer.

CHAPTER 50

EVICTED AND TOUGH DECISIONS

Did my life completely change when I started going to this 12-step program? Yes and No. My head began to clear and I felt better, because I learned that I had a disease marked by a physical allergy and a mental obsession. Now, I knew why I drove to that 7-11 everyday after school even though I loved those two boys more than life itself. On the other hand, I began to see the enormous damage I inflicted on my children and the guilt weighed on me like a giant boulder. I was sober and clean and could not swallow or smoke anything to lessen the burden.

By now, Ricky and Monti were teenagers. They were smoking pot and doing God only knows what else. They were skipping school and raising havoc on the street while I was working and going to meetings. One day, the rental realtor knocked on my door. I opened it and he shoved a piece of paper in my hand. "You need to be out in thirty days," he said and started to walk away.

"What, I ran after him, what are you talking about?" My head was spinning. I was stunned.

"Read it. I am sorry, but you have to leave." With that, he got into his car and drove away leaving me with a rolled up piece of paper in my trembling hand. I opened it. It was a petition signed by everyone in the neighborhood except a police officer who lived two doors away and knew me. It said that my kids were making too much noise and that the people wanted us out of this neighborhood. I was three months sober. I had no credit because there was no bill money after paying rent, food, utilities, school supplies, and clothes for the boys. I owed a huge hospital bill among others. I couldn't use El Monti Street as a reference because of the petition, so when I got the eviction notice, I was petrified. I called several rental agencies, but no one would rent to me. In addition, I was constantly calling the school to make sure my kids were there. I wasn't getting their report cards because they would skip school, get to the mailbox first, and steal the cards. I was frantic about Monty because he was sneaking out the window at night hanging out with college kids in dangerous places where he could be hurt. All their friends hung out at my house, and caused trouble in the neighborhood. One night, my front door slammed open and there was Darren and another kid, Bruce. Bruce was in handcuffs. "Gail, "Darren said breathless from running, you have to take the handcuffs off him. The cops arrested him for stealing at 7-11. They put him in the back of the police car, went in to talk to the store manager, so I snuck down the bank, opened the door, and let him out."

"What, are you crazy?" I said, I can't do that, and don't you realize that the police know you hang out here? This is the first place they will come looking. I opened the back door and said, "I'm sorry, Bruce, but you either let me call the police, or you have to leave."

They both went flying out the back door, and within thirty minutes, the police were knocking on my door. For once, I told them the truth. Later, I learned that this boy made it to his brother's house, and he took him to his uncle's in Arizona. I called my sponsor and tried to stay sane.

Another time, while Darren was living with us, he and Ricky encountered a truck driver in the parking lot of Albertson's. The truck driver offered them a beer. Ricky said, "Darren, I don't think we should get in the truck."

"Ah, come on, man. He's got beer," Darren said as he climbed up on the passenger's side running board, opened the door, and got in. Ricky tried to get him to leave with him, but he would not. Ricky left. That night I woke up to someone screaming. I jumped out of bed. It was Darren yelling incoherently. I thought he had taken some bad drugs.

230

"Darren," I screamed as I shook him, "what did you take?" He just laid on the floor with his hands over his face moaning. By this time, Ricky and Monti were there. Finally, he was able to whisper something about the man in the truck. I picked him up, helped him to the couch, and held him while he cried. The boys went to their room, and the next thing I knew, they were out the door. I ran to the door and yelled after them, "Where are you going? It's midnight. You can't be running around this late." They did not stop. By now, I understood that this man had fed Darren beers until he passed out and then molested him. Darren woke in the middle of it, fought him off, rolled out the door, and ran all the way home. I called the police and helped Darren fill out a report. I was worried sick about the kids, but I couldn't leave Darren. The kids came in the door while the police officer was there. As the police went out the door headed to Albertson's parking lot, I said, "That pervert is probably long gone by now."

Ricky said, "I don't think so. He held up a knife. Monti and I just put holes in all his tires. He's not going anywhere." Ricky testified in court for Darren and the man went to prison. Darren ended up in the mental ward for six months. My heart hurt for him and my guilt grew because he was in my charge while this happened.

In meetings, I was hearing about serenity and peace, but my life was about as peaceful as a volcano and tornado going off at the same time. I called my sponsor everyday about what to do with my kids. They complained that I was home more when I drank. I was now more alert, so behavior that was acceptable when I was drinking was no longer acceptable. For the first time in a couple of years, I was becoming consistent with them and it threw them into a tailspin. Now, I was facing homelessness along with the rest of the chaos. I began to contemplate thoughts such as, if this is what sobriety has to offer, I don't want it. I thought, at least when I was drinking I always had a roof over our heads.

Usually when I called my sponsor, my words were "Hi, I'm fine, and good by." I did not like to talk on the telephone, but I was scared of drinking again, so I called everyday as she had told me to do. One day I braved up and told her the whole story about the eviction notice.

When I finished, she said, "Gail, do you know what I do for a living?"

"No," I replied, irritated because she wanted to talk about her, not me.

"I manage apartments."

"Oh," was all I could say.

"I have an opening. I want you to come down here tomorrow morning and fill out an application.

Slowly, I began to connect the dots, "Really, I appreciate that, but the truth is, I have bad credit. You won't be able to rent to me."

"Are you willing to make a pledge to me that you will pay every month no matter what?"

I was silent for a moment, too stunned to speak. "Yes, I said, yes, but can you really rent me the place."

"Gail, I will see you tomorrow," she responded. We hung up and I sat there looking out the window sobbing inside like a fool remembering a promise I read, *God will do for us what we cannot do for ourselves.* Something I lost while trudging through Hell was the ability to cry tears. I could feel pain. I could hurt inside with sobs, but no tears flowed. My sight was damaged physically and spiritually.

In June, we moved into the new place and by October of that year, my sponsor was telling me that if I didn't keep my kids in school, the owner would kick me out. Right after I left El Monty St., the realtor once again knocked on my door. He told me that someone had taken an axe and chopped up the garage and left untold damage. I told him that I was sorry that happened and hoped they caught who did it. Deep down, I knew who did it. I was becoming more and more concerned for my teenage boys. I knew they were drinking and doing drugs, and I did not know how to stop them. I feared a drug dealer would kill them or they would end up in juvenile hall. That night, after the new eviction threat, I called their father, told him what they were doing, and asked him if he would take them. Without hesitation, he said, "Yes." I loved these children with all my heart, and I knew they would be safer in the Adirondacks than in Oceanside, but guilt was wreaking havoc with my insides.

By now, I had called them separately into my bedroom and made ninth step amends to them. I told them I was so sorry for what I had done when I was drinking. Amazingly, they loved me but were understandably angry. How does one make up for leaving their children or dragging them through the insane world of alcohol and drug addiction? How does one make up for something like that? There came a time when I had to accept that I could never go back and change the past. I only had today, and so I began to pray for guidance with these children.

One day, I came home early and found the boys in the townhouse with their friends once again. It was a school day. I sat them down and told them that if there was one more day of skipping school or the landlord threatening to kick me out because of them, they were moving this time, not me. I would send them to their father or a foster home. It was their choice. They chose their father even though they did not believe it would ever happen. The next weekend Monti snuck out his window, went down to the beach, and was forced into a car at knifepoint. He was sporting a large Marijuana bud, which attracted some dangerous people who wanted it. I grounded him, and talked to him about the danger of hanging with these people. The next weekend, I learned that he went to a nearby park late at night where a man was recently murdered. I had told both kids not to go in that park.

I prayed for two weeks to God to tell me what to do even though I was skeptical of God. My sponsor told me to pray to her God, and I did. In the meantime, the owner knocked on my door and told me that there were five or six kids hanging around all day that day. I cried and pleaded for one more chance and she gave it to me.

I prayed again that night, and the next morning as soon as I awoke I heard *"The Voice."* It said, "You need to send Monti to his father or he will be killed." I knew with immediate conviction exactly what I had to do. For the first time in a long time, I was completely at peace with the action I was about to take with my children. That night, I told Monti he had to go to his father's in Tupper Lake, NY to live. Although my oldest son, Ricky, was into drugs, he was a homebody. He did not stray too far from home, and he had the same instinct I had, which told him when danger was near. I did not tell him he needed to go and explained to Monti how I knew something bad was going to happen to him if he stayed here. He had to go. I told Ricky that it was his choice to stay or go. I didn't like what he was into, but I wasn't worried about him being killed.

Ricky said, "Where my brother goes, I go." Five days later, they were sitting on a bus in Oceanside headed for New York. I will forever wear that angry, sad look they gave me as the bus drove out of the station. I hurt in every fiber of my body. After they were gone, I would hear their voices calling, "Mom," run to the door, open it, and stare into space. I missed them terribly but in my heart, I knew that I had made the right decision. That decision taught me about prayer and meditation—that prayer is the request and meditation is listening, so you can hear the answer. Now, I knew that *"The Voice"* I heard throughout my life was my high power. This God was not the childhood one that condemned me to Hell for ringing the church bells and missing mass on Sunday. This God did not sweat the small stuff. He forgave me, loved me, took my hand in his, and walked through the briars with me.

CHAPTER 51

FELLOWSHIP AND FORGIVENESS

After meetings, we all gathered at Coco's restaurant, drinking coffee until 2:00 AM, and I wondered why I could not sleep. By the time I got into recovery, I had almost stopped eating. I was stick thin. I began to gain weight, and though it took a year, the shakes finally subsided (though to this day when I get nervous, my hands shake).I sat in a speaker meeting every Monday night being awed by the magnificence of my fellow alcoholic's stories. One man who was a teacher shared a past about being a cruel angry man, yet, today he was one of the kindest men I knew. I learned what this disease took from people-- families, houses, sanity, health, dignity, and dreams. There was no discrimination—teacher, lawyer, street bum or priest, none were immune. I met them all in these hallowed rooms. I shook, cried, and learned that I was just one of the herd. Bees did sting, but there was an antidote and it was here. Soon, I was making coffee at my home group on Friday nights, learning about different levels of honesty, and helping others.

This search for honesty led to many talks with my sponsor. In the beginning, I hated my father for what he had done. I did the steps with my sponsor and I still hated him. My sponsor told me I had to pray for him. I told her that I didn't know if I believed in God. One day I did, and the next day, I did not. I would rationalize, I am going to these meetings; I am making the changes, not God, and still another day I would gaze at the magnificent ocean and think, that is God.

Since I didn't have my own God concept, my sponsor told me to get down on my knees and pray to her God that all good things I wished for myself would come to my father. I did not want to go back to the Hell I had come from, so I did what she said even though I didn't believe her, and I certainly did not want good things to happen to him.

In September of 1982, my mother called and told me that she and Dad were taking a trip around the United States and would arrive in California in December. I was frantic. I had not seen either of them since I was sober, and I did not want to see my father, but I could not tell my mother not to come. By now, I was trying to live as honestly as I could while maintaining my prayer for Dad. The dreaded day arrived when I received the call from Mom. They were parked in a campsite in Carlsbad, CA only a few miles from my house. The drive over was excruciatingly painful. Once during my sobriety, my father wrote me a letter, and I started shaking so hard I got sick and had to give it to my sponsor to open and read to me. What was going to happen when I saw him in person?

I pulled into the campsite, exited my car, and began to walk over to their campsite. In the distance, I saw my father look up pull himself up from the picnic table, and walk toward me. I began to tremble. I did not see my mother. As my father came closer, and I awaited the hot hate to seep through me, I was amazed that it was not there. Instead, I began to feel an overpower love for this slightly stooped mountain of man walking toward me. I could not believe it; the hate was gone! I ran to him and hugged him. He hugged me back and for the first time since I was a little girl, I knew it was okay to love this man. I did not have to hide my love or pretend that it wasn't there. He was my father and I was free to feel my own feelings about him. Later, sitting with him alone at the picnic table he said, "My biggest mistake was buying that bar. If I had it to do over, I would not do that again." That was my father's apology. This proud, strong, intelligent man came as far as he could come, and I accepted it. He never stopped drinking, but eventually slowed down to a couple of drinks a night. Through the next ten years, we had a good relationship. He had a stroke a couple of years later; I took him on trips to Canton, NY, where he grew up, to visit his old friends. One regret I carry with me is never attempting to take him to a meeting. He probably would not have gone, but I always wonder. This experience taught me the power of prayer and the freedom of forgiveness.

CHAPTER 52

LETTING GO AND MOVING ON

It was during the summer of 1981, that I decided to go to college. I had no clue how to do that or where to go, so I asked the teacher. He told me to go to the local college and talk to a counselor. The closest two-year college was Mira Costa College, so I drove there, spoke with a counselor, and that September, there I was on registration day, terrified, knowing I was stupid, but powered by sheer grit to go to school.

Going back to college had always been a dream I thought impossible. On this his first day, my fears ran the gamut with thoughts, of how did I think I could do this when I couldn't even find the right line for registration; I am just going to quit after a couple classes, and now everyone will know how stupid I really am. After shaking all day, and asking a million questions, I managed to leave the campus registered for college, beginning with remedial math and English classes. I was lost because I had been out of school for eighteen years; on the other hand, I was sober and determined. I learned that I could use facets of my personality negatively or positively. I was a stubborn, rebellious child who listened to my head and did what it told me to do. It blocked out my mother's voice, God's voice, and any other voice that interfered with what I wanted to do.

Once I started to grow up at 35 years old, I used that stubbornness to make myself sit tediously at the table into the early morning learning how to do fifth grade fractions. Fractions happened during my brain tumor missed school days. Now, I learned that I loved this new world of chalkboards, books, and learning. I was astounded at how much I did not know, and I wanted to learn everything.

That summer after my first year of sobriety, I decided to camp across country. I was going to the Grand Canyon, spend a few nights here and a few nights there, and end up in Virginia at my brother, Mike's house. Instead, I got in the car, drove an average of 90 miles an hour, slept two hours in a rest stop, and arrived at my brother's house three days later. Slowing down and seeing the sights had not arrived yet. I was still in fast forward gear. I set my sights on a goal, and like a deer in headlights, I went straight to that goal. Mike went to a meeting with me in Harrisonburg, and then he went to several more, while His wife, Sherry, attended a different program. I left their home so happy to have spent time with them, but fearful of my brother's impending first few weeks of sobriety. I had learned that people die from alcohol withdrawal, and I prayed that he would get medical help even though he refused to do so while I was there.

When I returned to California, I brought my sister, Sheryl, and her son, Jason, with me. She was running away from her abusive husband, and I was happy to have her with me. She was so beautiful inside and outside. She had long blonde hair, bright blue eyes, beautiful olive skin, and a smile that lit up her whole face. When we got to California, she started going to meetings with me, but eventually her husband talked her into flying back to him. I was sorry to see her go, but I knew that was her journey. All I could do was pray for her, call Mom and ask her to be ready for her to come home when she hit her bottom with this man's abuse. I just prayed the bottom came before he killed her.

I loved college and soon decided I wanted to be an English teacher. Shockingly, I did very well in school, making the dean's list the whole way through Mira Costa. I transferred to San Diego State and began my coursework for my Bachelor's degree. Every step of the way was terrifying and exciting at the same time; however, I still had not reached a level of self-honesty that would allow me to see that I was intelligent enough to receive the high grades recorded on my record. Skeptical thoughts continued to haunt me that the professors felt sorry for me, or the classes I took were the easy ones, and that is why I scored such high grades.

One required course was an intense poetry class. Poetry was something I had written all my life. I had poems from childhood, poems with beer stains and tearstains on them, and poems about my children. One of our assignments was to write about an emotional time in our life. I fretted and sat for hours trying to get words on paper but unable to do the assignment. Through the years, I had excelled at burying feelings and shutting off emotions. Finally, one night I began to write, and it felt like the pen was moving by itself. I wrote a poem about signing the telegram after Stewart's death. The words were steeped in anger. When I gave it to the teacher for editing, he pointed out that I only told part of the story. He wanted to know something positive about this man. There had to be something positive, or I would not have married him. I was furious at the teacher. Didn't he understand? How could he; he probably grew up in an Ozzie and Harriet home like most teachers. I got home, sat down at the table, and stared at the paper in front of me. How could I write anything positive when I was barely able to think about this time in my life? I wanted to write a different one. The professor told me I had to finish this one, and I needed this class to graduate. I was in a dilemma and did not know what to do. My body still shook when I saw pictures of wells, or violence on TV. I still ducked when a man near me lifted his arm over his head for any reason.

Soon, I began to see everyone as different from me. I felt sad and walked around San Diego State Campus feeling isolated. I went to meetings and tried to turn it all over to God, but I became more and more silent and more and more withdrawn. I visited the campus priest and began to attend mass again, and though I began to see the beauty in the church teachings, I still went home and dealt with the increasingly violent nightmares. One day, I mustered up all my nerve and opened the door to the campus counseling office. I told the secretary what I was experiencing and she scheduled an appointment for me the next day with a male counselor. I was leery of a male, but he was the only one available. I could not be alone with men. I went out in groups. I did not have a man in my house for many years, and I did not develop true feelings for another for many years; not that I did not see men; I did, at their house, on my terms, so they could only see a little of me.

I went to Mr. Mitchell for a couple of sessions, and he told me we needed to talk about the abuse in my past. I had talked a little about my father and boyfriends, but not about Stewart. I told him about my father, my childhood molestations, beatings by Kenneth, and finally my near death experience with Stewart. Sometimes we did this through hypnosis, mostly; we did this through talk therapy with me curled up in the fetal position suffering the pain of a thousand nights of tragedy rolled into this moment. Sometimes I ran to his office knowing I would be safe from the demons in my mind, and sometimes I reluctantly showed up even though that is the last place I wanted to be. The nightmares increased during this time. I woke up screaming, shaking, and staring at the bedroom walls in my little cottage in San Diego. I had no television because school took all my money, so I would get up, read a spiritual book, sometimes go back to sleep and sometimes not.

Mr. Mitchell asked me if I wanted something to deal with my depression. I remembered hearing in the meetings that we were not to take any mood or mind-altering drugs. I said, "Can I just come here and talk and go to my meetings?"

He told me I had something called Post Traumatic Stress Syndrome and that he understood about my wish not to medicate myself. He told me to share all of this with my sponsor and to continue to see him once a week. I did what he said and soon my sponsor knew the whole story. I did write that poem that led me to uncovering, discovering, and discarding what I no longer needed in my life.

This poem led me down a path of forgiveness that sings joy in my heart today. Do I blame Stewart? No, he was a victim from the time he was a little boy. Alcoholism was rampant in his family and he was not to escape this dreaded disease. When he entered the Navy and went to Vietnam, he was in his element. He felt comfortable and he requested to go back three times and did. He spent six years fighting. He was wounded twice. Do I forgive him? Absolutely. Have I forgotten? No. It will always be there in a sudden noise, a rumbling yell, fireworks, or a glance at an old well. The shining light falls on forgiveness, which emanates from me when I think of him—his turquoise eyes, his familiar gait as he walked in his green pants, military boots, and flannel shirt. I remember his tender touch, his kindness to my boys, and his boyish smirk. I loved this man and wrote several poems about him. Thank God for forgiveness. It lets me see the spirit in him just as I see the spirit in a beautiful sugar maple lain by lightning, blackened and decayed once majestic, standing strong in blunt force winds, now awaiting its new life. I wonder where he is, this beautiful man who walks in someone else today. He did his time and he is at peace wherever he goes. His spirit is forever in my heart.

CHAPTER 53

TURNING FEAR INTO POWER

One day, I was sitting in an Alano Club in San Diego. I saw a tall light blonde haired woman stroll through the door. She wore a halter-top, breasts half hanging out, short shorts and flip-flops. She had an angular face with high cheekbones; light blue eyes and she reminded me of a Nordic princess. After the meeting, I introduced myself. She had just moved here from Hollywood and her name was Lillian. We became instant friends. She had dated a member of the band called, "Dio," and her good friend was their manager. She knew many stars such as Rod Stewart; she laughed a lot, was crazy like me, and liked to have fun.

One day at school, I saw a flyer announcing something called a firewalk. By now, I was reading books like, _The Course in Miracles,_ taking classes in metaphysics, and attending church where a renowned minister, Terry Cole Whitaker, preached about love, and forgiveness. I was curious about this firewalk, so I called and found out it was a seminar given by a man named Tony Robbins. He also taught something called Neurolinguistic Programming. My new sober life had infused in me a wild zest for living. I wanted to see, do, and learn everything. I was ecstatic. I was going to walk on fire! I believed that if I could get sober, I could do anything. I was still very pessimistic, untrusting, and fearful, though I was progressing." The day I saw the flyer, I went home and called Lillian. "Hey, Lil, want to go to a seminar with me?

"Sure, is it at the church?"

"No, its in a hotel."

"Really, what is it, Gail?"

"We're going to walk on fire," I said enthusiastically.

"What, are you crazy? What are you talking about?" I explained to her about Tony Robbins and how he taught a seminar on how to turn fear into power and he used firewalking as a metaphor for this theory. I still had tremendous fear and self-doubt even though I was getting better each day; consequently, I pounced on anything that had the word, "Fear," in it.

"I'll go, but I'm not walking on fire" was her reply. We signed up and a month later, there we were sitting in a huge meeting room with fifty other people anxiously waiting for Tony Robbins to come on stage. I heard Patti LaBelle's voice blasting in the background with *" New Attitude."* The atmosphere was lively, positive, and highly charged, all the things I loved. Suddenly, a giant of a man walked across the stage in three steps. My heart stopped. He was gorgeous from his shiny black hair, English nose, all the way to his long legs. He was about six foot five with hands big enough to wrap around a basketball. When he smiled, his white teeth lit up his whole face, and when he talked, intelligence burst out of him like fireworks. I listened to every word and loved everything he was saying because it sounded like I felt—happy, positive, and grateful to be alive. Around 7:00 PM, he led us out to the parking lot where he had a pile of wood. He lit the wood, created a large bonfire, and told us that at midnight we would come out and walk on the coals. Lillian was still refusing to do it, and I was saying, "Yes, you will, and why not, we almost killed ourselves, didn't we?"

"Yes, she replied, and now I want to live." That evening, we listened to Tony, did some exercises and meditation and at midnight, the group went outside in the hotel parking lot. When I saw the hot red coals strung out in a twelve-foot path, I started to recoil. I thought, no one could do that without burning the hell out of her feet. This is not possible. The next thing I knew, there was Tony standing barefoot in the middle of the coals talking to us. Then, he reached down and picked up one of the hot coals.

248

My mouth dropped open and I heard Lillian say, "No way, no damn way I'm doing this." I, too, backed up, changing my mind about walking. Soon, people began walking across the coals with Tony. I thought again, as I did when I was trying to get sober and watching other people do it, if they can do it, I can do it. I said aloud, "Okay, God, come on, we're doing this." I walked up and stood in line still shaking, and soon found myself standing next to Tony.

"You ready," he said flashing that enormous smile.

"I'm ready as I'm ever going to be," I shouted. Tony took my hand and we walked across the coals. He told me to repeat the mantra, "cool moss, cool moss," and look up. He taught the concept that looking down placed your mindset in your body and your emotions, while looking up, placed you in your mind. He used the analogy of a person who is sad, looks down at his feet when he walks. In addition, in the seminar he asked us to spell words by looking down and then again, looking up. We did better when we looked up because this was the analytical memory working. Therefore, looking down at the coals conveyed the reality of hot burning coals; looking away allowed the power of the mind to overcome matter. I took a step out onto the coals. It felt like popcorn under my feet as I gingerly put one foot in front of the other. Two of his assistants, stood at the end of the walk. They took my arms and told me to step into a pan of cold water placed at the end of the walk. I did that and then an immense euphoria overcame me, and I was screaming, "I did it, I did it!" We were all screaming, jumping, and hugging each other. We turned and watched the rest of the people come across joining in their excitement at the end. Lillian was still standing on the other side waiting for everyone to finish. I kept motioning her to come, and she kept nodding her head, no. Then, she lifted up her arms in surrender, walked over and became the last one to do the firewalk that night. She, too, was thrilled at what she had done. We finished the seminar and I learned some tricks called "anchors" to use whenever I needed strength.

Now, I had my meetings, sober friends, classes, and a new I can do it attitude. I became a Tony Robbins assistant and for the next couple of years helped many people across the hot coals. Tony met a beautiful woman and married her in his castle in Del Mar, Ca. The marriage ceremony was a spectacular event involving beautiful white horses pulling a grand carriage all the way to and from the castle. I was loving life and great events were yet to pass.

CHAPTER 54

THE RIPPLE EFFECT

My fifth year of sobriety was highlighted by a phone call in the middle of the night and another amazing road trip.

Sadly, my son, Ricky, was now a drug addict and alcoholic living on the streets of San Diego. He was heavy into his addiction and no longer working. He had come home a couple of times, but always left, or I made him leave because I could not tolerate his life style. I lived in a different world now, and my heart hurt for him, but I knew I had done all I could. I started attending another 12-step program dealing with the families of alcoholics. It centered on a philosophy of "Tough Love." Normally, when either of my sons asked for money, I gave them whatever I could spare. My sponsor in this new program said that from now on the answer was always "No" when Ricky asked for money. Sometimes he would call and tell me he had no food. I felt the familiar fear creep into my heart and pulse through my veins, but I began to say, "No." It was so hard, so foreign. I would say "No," pick up the phone, and call my sponsors crying because everything in me as a mother told me to help my child, so he would not starve. I would ask him if he was willing to go to meetings and his answer was to hang up. The last time I saw him, he was cornstalk thin. It scared me, and I prayed repeatedly for his safety, and always told him that if he wanted help, to call.

That call came in the middle of a summer night in 1986. I said, "Hello."

Then I heard the magic words I had waited so long to hear," Mom, I need help." I could not breathe. I could not believe this was Ricky asking for help. Hope was still my enemy. I said, "Ricky, do you mean you want to come home?"

"Yes, Mom, can I?"

"What's going on?" I asked bracing for the answer.

"They're all after me and the dolls heads are turning around."

"What dolls heads are turning around?"

"At the bottom of the bed, they're all spinning around." My mind raced. He had to be high. Was he serious? I was waiting for the "I need money" line. Instead, he told me that even his best friend was out to get him and that he had planted drugs in his car.

I said, "Ricky, you can come home, but only if you are willing to go to a meeting every night." I waited for the dull buzz in my ear as he slammed the phone down. I had tried discussing his addiction with him before. I had gone to drug programs, gathered literature, and left it on his coffee table. The discussion about "Ricky I think you are addicted to drugs and alcohol" did not go well. He became insanely angry and forced me out the door. I did manage to leave the literature, and he probably promptly threw it out.

The next words I heard made my heart stop. "Ok, Mom, I'll do anything."

"Where are you?

"In Oceanside."

"Can you drive here?"

"Yes, I have the Bible with me," he said.

"You what?"

"I have the Bible. It will protect me." That did not comfort me. In his state, it scared me. I knew he was high, so I offered to come and get him. He told me that he could drive his car. I did not want to anger him, so I told him that if he wasn't there in an hour, I would head up to Oceanside. Forty-five minutes later, he pulled up in front of the house. He had the Bible in his hand. It got him safely to San Diego. When he came through the door, I had to control my reaction. He was stick thin, whiter than snow, and his once big blue eyes donned red rims. He had not slept for days. We hugged for what seemed like hours, and we both cried. Something inside told me that I had made the right decision to let him come. He slept for three days with the Bible under his arm. I called Harvey, a long time sober alcoholic addict and asked him what to do. I was worried because he had slept for two days and would not eat. He told me to let him sleep. He related that Ricky had probably not slept in days because of the drugs he was taking.

Finally, on the third day, he woke up and ate. That night we started going to meetings. I introduced him to the men, and he soon got a sponsor and became involved in the program. The Bible stayed with him all night. It was his higher power and it gave him courage to do the things he felt he could not do alone until he received more tools to add to this wonderful book. The winds were blowing my way, and I was sailing along in sobriety, determined to see and do as much as I could in this new world. By the next year, I was ready for another road trip.

CHAPTER 55

THERE ARE NO COINCIDENCES

The beauty of the United States and its people marked the second road trip. I stopped in Sedona, Arizona for one night, pitched my tent, went to a 5:30 meeting, and stayed one week. I met a man in the local diner, and he took me to an old mining town and many other sites. I went up a mountain in a jeep with tires blown up like balloons, saw one of the seven sacred spots in the world, panned for gold, and hiked the craggy cliffs. I met a man in town who gave me a story he had been writing and asked me to edit it (by now I had graduated from college). I took the story back to my tent and spent the afternoon reading and editing.

I swam in the Verde River and hiked in the high desert. I loved that little town nestled under mammoth red rocks. I visited a chapel designed within the rocks. The church's cross was perched high on the ridge, shining brilliantly in the night sky. It was 1987 and this was a little town with a few unique buildings surrounded by magnificent natural beauty.

I drove on up the winding road into the magnificent Grand Canyon. I was in awe as I scoured this gift from God. On a ridge halfway down the trail, I got down on my knees, thanked God for this magnificent painting and left my sobriety chip in the loose red soil. On my drive up to the Grand Canyon, I saw a place that rented teepees. I thought to myself, Wow, I've never slept in a teepee. I pulled over and rented it for $10.00. That night I pulled my sleeping bag out, laid it on the ground, and slept in a teepee almost as big as a house. I was so thrilled with this life that I just wanted to experience everything I could. Life had passed me by while I was sitting at my kitchen table looking at one more bottle of beer in front of me depressed by the four walls of my existence. Now here I was seeing my country in her beauty and glory, living outside where I loved to be.

I drove on to Amarillo, Texas where I woke up one morning to the most God awful honking sound I had ever heard. I jumped up, and looked around. I did not see anything or anyone, but I had my hatchet in my hand. Soon, I started the campfire, went down to the river to fill my coffee pot, and heard it again. It was not a coyote or anything else I had ever heard, but it was getting closer. I thought, well the fire will scare it away. Soon the fire was blazing, and I set my coffee pot on the iron grate waiting for that wonderful smell to permeate my space. I took out my meditation books and began to read and then meditate. I heard the honking sound one more time. I quickly drank my coffee and packed up my gear. On my way out of the campsite, I stopped and asked the caretakers about the sound. They told me it was a peacock and that they do not know how it got there, but it ran wild in the woods. I was thrilled with all of the firsts I was experiencing. That was the first time I ever heard a peacock. Life was good and it just kept getting better. I began to learn the wisdom of planning the journey but not the outcome; however, hard knocks lurked right around the corner, and I was not ready.

It took me two and a half weeks to get to Virginia. America is such a beautiful country and every state I went through added to it. I spent a day in the Appalachians and went to Dollywood, Pigeon Hollow, and Gatlinburg. I climbed the steep mountains of West Virginia and was amazed how the tiny houses were tucked away among the trees along the way. On the final stretch of my journey to my brother's house in Harrisonburg, I traveled the same roads Mike Tracy and I had traveled so many years before when we were young and in love. We were so happy and so excited about our life together with our two boys. My stomach tightened and my chest hurt thinking about my life with Mike. Crying was still not there on the outside. I only cried on the inside and it hurt. I went by the Dutch Pantry where I used to work. I saw him coming in through the door to have a cup of coffee. I remembered how just seeing him pull in the driveway or walk through a door lit me up inside like a Christmas tree. I recalled our last conversation many years ago, ending with Mike hanging up on me, hurt and angry because I told him not to come to California.

I pulled into the gravel driveway leading up to my brother's house. It was an old farmhouse with a front porch and beautiful lush green lawn with bushes of pink and white flowers peeking out from the wooded perimeter. I walked up the worn wood steps, through the front door, met my brother, Mike, in the kitchen, and hugged him. I let go, stood back, and heard footsteps coming through the dining room. I looked up and there he was--blonde brown hair cut short, looking at me with a half grin. I froze. I scanned his face for some hint of emotion. My body trembled and my hands shook so badly I held them behind me. Suddenly, Mike began walking towards me and in two long strides; we were wrapped in each other's arms. We pulled apart, looked at each other and as if without will, our lips met and he kissed me long and hard. It was as if we had never parted. The love for him filled me up completely and I whispered in his ear, "I love you."

"I love you, too, he said, always have, and always will." By this time, my brother and his wife, Sherry, had left the room. I looked at his face—the same blue eyes, same face more weathered than when I had left almost ten years before. He told me he had married but was separated from his wife, and he hadn't had a drink in four years. We spent most of that summer together, riding his Harley around Virginia, and then to Long Lake. Mike dedicated his love and life to me and asked me to live with him. I readily agreed, knowing his divorce proceedings were in progress.

Because I had known this man since childhood and lived with him for many years, I knew he loved me. It didn't work before, but he was older, wiser, and much calmer now. I knew this was God's will because how could two people still be in love after ten years of being apart? Equally important, was the coincidence that Mike was also sober. I reasoned that God had given us this second chance, and I was not letting it float by me.

Many evenings, we sat out on the porch and joked about how we would grow old together, sit in our rocking chairs, and hold hands. I applied for a teaching job in the Winchester and Harrisonburg area. Frederick County hired me to teach English as a Second Language at Bass Hoover Elementary school in Stephens City.

Throughout the years, my children had stayed in contact with Mike. He was their step Dad and they both had lived with him at times during the summer months.

Mike worked in Maryland running heavy equipment building rock walls to prevent erosion in the Chesapeake Bay. I found an apartment in Winchester, on Wilson Boulevard, flew back to San Diego, CA, packed my clothes, gave stuff away, and said a tearful good by to Ricky who was now almost two years sober. I watched him out of my rearview mirror as I drove away, standing in front of my cottage waving good by with tears in his eyes. It broke my heart, but he was sober and had many friends now, a job, and new red pickup truck.

On the airplane ride home, I gazed out the window at the Virginia landscape. The trees looked like green lollipops stuck in green fields of grass, so different from the brown of the Rocky Mountains out West. I was thrilled about living in the East again, starting a new job, and reuniting with my soul mate. "Thank you God," I whispered. The plane landed at National Airport in DC. I found my car in the parking lot, pulled out into traffic, construction, and morning mayhem, and immediately became lost. I called Mike, and he gave me directions.

Two and a half hours later, I pulled into the parking lot of the apartment. I ran up the stairs, opened the door, and yelled, "Mike, I'm home." It was strange that he didn't answer because he was home when I called for directions. "Mike," I called again as I glanced at bouquet of red roses on the table. I smiled and thought, how romantic. I walked over, sniffed the roses, and noticed a piece of paper under the vase.

I picked it up and read the following words, "I am sorry, I can't do this. I love you. Good by, Gail" It was signed, "Love, Mike." I could not believe what I was reading. I scanned the message again. My brain stopped dead. I threw the note down on the counter and ran to the closet. All his clothes were gone. I looked around the bedroom. Nothing. It was as if he had never been there. The place screamed of silence. I felt all the blood drain from my body. There was no furniture because we were going the next the day to get furniture. I sank down on the carpet, screamed, and begged God to bring him back. I thought, there must be a mistake. This cannot be. I was so sure this was the right thing. God, why did you do this to me?

I stayed in that tomb for three days only leaving to go to the pay phone trying to call him. He would not answer his telephone. I was frantic. I did not know what to do. I had no telephone, no bed; I did not know one person in Winchester, and I had not been to a meeting in three days. I called my sponsor, lamenting my predicament to her. I called Rick, a wonderful man I had dated in California. I would say to Rick, "Say something about God," and he would tell me how God did not give us any more than we could handle. I would reply, "If God, puts one more grain of sand on my heart, it will crack." My body was wracked with pain, while tears remained locked inside my heart. There was no sleep, no peace, no joy.

On the third or fourth night of not sleeping on the carpet (I still had no furniture), I decided to return to California. I did not know anyone here. All I had were memories of Mike in this

259

apartment, so at 1:00 AM I began loading the car. By 4:00 AM, the car was packed, and I was ready to leave. As I was putting my backpack in the car, I suddenly remembered that I had mailed the rest of my belongings to Winchester, and they were arriving within the next two days. Thoughts of my new job flashed through my brain, followed by a reminder that I had a job, an apartment, and only days ago, was in love with the beautiful landscape I witnessed from the airplane.

At 5:00 AM that morning, I walked to the telephone booth and called Rick. He answered. He always did. No matter what time I called, he answered. He had fallen in love with me, but he respected my decision to remain his friend no matter what. He was and is one of the most spiritual men I have ever known. Every time I heard his voice, it calmed me.

"Hello Gail," he said already knowing I was the only one who would be calling him at this hour.

"Rick, my car is packed. I was headed back to California, but realized that I mailed the rest of my things to this address. Those boxes won't get here for at least two more days. What should I do?" I was shaking from little sleep, no food, no meetings, and grief.

"Gail, if it were me, I would stay there long enough to at least receive my possessions. You need to find the meetings there. Have you gone to any?"

"No, I whispered, "I can't." "I can't see people."

"Then go to the damn meeting and shut your eyes, but go to a meeting!" I pulled the telephone away and looked into it. He had never spoken to me like that. "Gail, you don't have to decide anything right now except where to go to a meeting."

"Ok, Rick, say something God to me," I whimpered.

"God is going to kick your ass if you drink! Do you want to go back to that old life?"

"No," I replied.

"Then promise God and me you will go to a meeting." Before I got off the telephone, I promised him I would do that. I called the hot line and they told me there was a noon meeting downtown. I decided to walk to the meeting. Every street I crossed and every car I saw coming toward me, I secretly wished would hit me. I walked slowly, never changing my gait whether a car was coming or not. I did not have the guts to commit suicide nor the will to prevent it from happening by car. Ironic, I thought, I remember that night so long ago when I cut my wrist, wanting to die over this same man. Then I remembered the words, "Gail, no man is worth dying for."

At the corner of two intersecting streets, I saw the white wood building. I climbed up the steps, opened the door, and walked in. I saw people sitting around a table. It reminded me of the table at the Oceanside Alano Club. The familiar aroma of fresh brewed coffee hit me. I walked in, poured myself a cup of coffee, and sat in the chair against the back table facing the door.

I felt like a newcomer walking into my first meeting, but I could breathe for the first time in three days. I don't remember the topic, but I raised my hand and shared that I had just moved here and my boyfriend left me. I shared that I did not know anyone, and now, I wanted to die. Then, a man with brown eyes and slicked back brown hair began to speak. He had a deep southern accent. He shared about his experience in early sobriety with a relationship break up, but he eventually met the love of his life, prayed with her, and married her. Immediately, I felt the black begin to lift. I felt the warm ray of hope begin to blanket me.

It always seemed ironic to me that in spite of my hurtful experience with men, these two men, Rick and this man, saved me from myself, and I am forever grateful to them. It is said in our writings that we never know how many lives we touch. I wonder if they know how they touched mine. A wonderful woman named Barbara came up to me after the meeting and asked me to go to coffee with her. She bought me lunch and I ate for the first time since I had walked into that empty apartment.

The next morning, I took Mike's credit card and bought furniture. I was by no means a spiritual giant yet, but I made the decision to stay. He did contact me after a couple of weeks and was almost grateful I had bought the furniture, because of his guilt. He came to the apartment a couple of times telling me he loved me and could not stay away. However, soon he would leave, breaking my heart again. I was powerless over the nearness of him and unable to let him go. I kept going to meetings, got a sponsor, and prayed for the courage to change the things I could. Eventually, with great sorrow, I told him he could not come back. I swore as I walked away that I would never go there again.

CHAPTER 56

TRUDGING THE RELATIONSHIP ROAD

After deciding to stay, I focused on my job, teaching English as a Second Language to elementary school students. I was the first ESL teacher in Frederick County, and the only materials we had were the ones I had salvaged from teaching in California. At first, it was overwhelming because it was so different. In California, I taught adults in the summer and middle school in the winter. I only had four students that first year in Virginia, but with no materials, it was a challenge. I made it through and eventually, more students came, and we hired another teacher. I loved this job from the start. I held the secret of where I came from tight in my heart and lived in gratitude for where I was.

One night, the telephone rang. I picked it up. "Hello Beautiful." It was Mike, and I immediately felt the familiar adrenalin zing rushing through my body.

"Hi Mike."

"Just calling to see what you are doing."

"I'm teaching now. Where are you?"

"I'm building a new house. It's almost finished. I'd like to show it to you."

"Mike, I'm happy for you," I said, and I was. He had come from rough beginnings, and I was proud of him for working hard and achieving the American dream. "I am proud of you, Mike, but I don't think it is a good idea for me to see you."

"Why, he said, I'm not asking you to go to bed with me, just look at my house."

After a few minutes, he talked me into it and I found myself saying, Okay, Mike, I would love to see it." He gave me directions and the next morning I went to West Virginia to meet him. As always, we slammed together like opposite ends of a magnet, and, as always, he was separated from his wife.

When we said good by, we professed our love for each other, laughing about being 80 years old in our rocking chairs together on the porch.

Driving down Route 50 that afternoon, I experienced a change in my perception. For the first time, I saw our relationship for what it was—old friends and an occasional rendezvous. Each time I saw him, I thought it was the last, yet for years, we blew into each other's lives like a hot summer wind. I melted when I saw his crooked smile, and tingled when his arms went around me, but as I pulled into my driveway, this time, I knew that there would be no rocking chairs for us.

Mike remained a stepfather to my children, so most of the years I knew where he was. Eventually, both boys moved to Virginia and Mike contacted them every Christmas and came to dinner a few times.

On one of his visits, he told me that a month before I came to Virginia that first time, he had drunk a beer after four years of sobriety. By the time I came in June, he was contemplating going back to his old drinking life. He knew he could not drink if he lived with me, so he chose alcohol over me. I felt better because I understood that decision. I was not resentful toward him even though he lied about the divorce proceedings and went back to his wife. I thought, "I learned my lesson on that one, God, and that will never happen again."

Two years later I met Frank at a local restaurant after a meeting. He was sitting in the chair next to me at Big Boy's Restaurant. He was Robert Redford handsome with his light blonde hair and big blue eyes, and I was infatuated. After several encounters, one of us asked the other to go to Shoneys for coffee. That is how it started. My intentions were always sincere and pure. What happened was not always what I intended. Frank was quiet, secretive, gentle, and funny. We went to the same meetings, and before long, we were going out to coffee. For a long time, we were friends, but in truth, I was rocking inside just being near him. He talked about how his marriage did not work, and I listened mesmerized by his boyish face, and his neediness. He was sad and depressed much of the time, and I thought, I could help him. I could brighten up his day, I thought, and soon was brightening up his nights with *the voice* screaming at me the whole way, "No, Gail, there will be consequences."

I remember saying, "I know their will be consequences, but this is worth it." Incredibly, wouldn't you know, he too was "separated" In addition, he told me that he was living in his van. I couldn't have him living in a van when I had a perfectly good townhouse, so he moved in with me. That is when I found out from a lovely blonde lady who visited me two days later that they were not really legally separated. This lady was his wife. I confronted him and after a week of seeing her and seeing me, he left her. The guilt piled on me like a heavy pack. Soon, I discovered he was depressed, a gambler, and allergic to work. He was also funny, smart, kind, loving and a great dancer. We laughed and had lot of fun together. I am sure his wife was not having fun while I was twirling and whirling around the dance floor with her husband.

Our relationship lasted for 2 ½ years and he did get a divorce, but he was always depressed, wanted to stay in the pool hall, and complained constantly about his job. I wasn't laughing anymore, and finally, I broke up with him. He met another woman that same day at a picnic and started dating her. I was devastated. I wanted him back. Consequences ripped in like a tidal wave.

One night, at the Friday night meeting when I was eight years sober, I saw a young couple with an infant. I began to feel an overwhelming happiness for that baby. That child would never have to witness what my children did. She would grow up in a sober home. My eyes began to sting, and I felt water on my cheeks. I reached up and touched it. They were tears! I was crying. For the first time, in years, I was able to cry! I rushed into the bathroom, sat on the toilet, and cried. It was a miracle. I was on the brink of normal and loving it!

I went back to a counselor, spent many sessions crying, and grieving over the losses in my life. I screamed, lost weight, lost sleep, called my sponsor, and called Frank about the new woman. I told him how much I hated her, and how she was all wrong for him. Six months later, he married her.

During this period, I wrote plays, and we performed them at our annual conventions. They were large three act plays, which included many scenes and stories from people I had met in the meeting rooms.

I also wrote plays and directed a drama club for my students. It was so rewarding, and I was so proud of these children who learned to overcome their fear, get up on stage, and perform beyond their greatest expectations.

About two years after this long relationship with Frank, I was chairing a meeting when a large man walked through the door. He was as tall as the door, with curly black hair hanging to his shoulders, a straight Charlton Heston nose, and an arrogant swagger. I thought, "Oh, a wild whacky newcomer," and went on talking to my friend sitting next to me. I started the meeting and we went around the table sharing. When it came to him, I expected him to pass or make an unintelligible verbal statement, but when he opened his mouth and spoke, I knew in an instant he was not a newcomer, and was highly intelligent, and that quality in a man drew me in like a magnet. I listened to what he had to say, and after the meeting, I spoke to him. He said he had five years sober, so I asked him to speak at my home speaker meeting.

"Sure, I would love to," he replied. "I just need to make sure I can get a ride."

266

"Why, I asked. I knew he had five years. Why did he need a ride?"

"I lost my driver's license. It's embarrassing after five years, but I owe too many fines."

Something clicked in my brain about this. I had learned that when people talk and the logic is missing, there is a lie somewhere. On the other hand, I was mesmerized by this man's ability with the English language. It trumped no license, on the run from bill collectors, and discovering that his meeting attendance was close to zero for the last three years. So, instead of running away like a speeding bullet, I said, "Would you like to go to the movies sometime?"

He responded, "Sure, really, you want to go with me?" Even he was shocked that I asked him. That should have been a clue. When I arrived in Middletown to pick him up, he had cut his hair and bought me a box of chocolates. I was touched, and so began my relationship with this man who by all appearances looked like he just rolled out of a garbage can, but I loved talking to him and listening to him. His name was Alex and we began dating, going to meetings together, and sharing how we were so much alike. Soon, we moved in together, and immediately, there were problems. I liked the country; he liked the city; I had helped him get his license back; he was ungrateful; I suggested he go to school, thinking that was a good thing; he resented me for suggesting it. I had long-term sobriety by this time, and though he had had those five years, they had not been years of working on himself, so there was a huge gap in our perception of the world.

Alex and I did many things together, including going on a cruise to the Bahamas. We had a great time, and I loved being with him. One summer, I took him to the Adirondacks. He loved fishing, and I knew he would love catching bass and pike. He did. At that time, my father and mother were both suffering from Emphysema. Alex went to the nursing home with me to meet my father. We returned home on Sunday because I had to start a class on Monday at Eastern Mennonite University. This class was an intense weeklong course I needed in order to finish my masters. On Wednesday morning, Alex called me and said, "I have something bad to tell you. Your father died."

The news floored me, "Oh, my God, but he was fine just a week ago," I said as the numbness began to permeate my body.

"I know. I couldn't believe it either, but your mother called here. You need to call her."

"Okay, I will, thanks" I said. I hung up and called my mother. Dad had fallen in the nursing home and broken his pelvis. They took him to Saranac Lake Hospital where he died that night. He was eighty years old. "Mom, I'm in the middle of this class, but I will come home. What are the arrangements?"

"No, Gail, do not come home. The week before, I had expressed to her how important this class was to me. "He would not want you to do this. You know he was so proud of you for going to college. Please don't leave your class. That is not what he would have wanted you to do, Gail."

"I guess," I said. I remembered how he bragged to everyone about his daughter going to college. I had disappointed him immensely when I dropped out many years ago. When I went back, he was proud. Mom told me there was just going to be a memorial and the best thing I could do for him was to finish what I was doing. I went to class and felt like I was outside looking in. I could not stop thinking about him. In my room that night, I cried for him, this man I had loved and hated my whole life who never had a chance to be all he could have been because alcohol took away the best part of him. I studied, listened, and did my best. I came out with an A in that course. Once home, I grieved silently, touched by triggers.

One night about a week after his death, I was watching TV and Matlock came on. As soon as Andy Griffith walked onto the set, I started crying. Dad always reminded me of him, his build, hair, and mannerisms. Alex walked out of the room.

Now, Alex and I were constantly fighting. I was resentful that he had no empathy for me, and how I was feeling, and he was confused as to why I would feel anything after what Dad had done to me. Two weeks after my father died, Alex came home and told me he had found a place. I was confused because I did not know he was looking for one. I started crying immediately. He sat down on the couch with me one last time, held me while I sobbed in his arms for twenty minutes, and then, walked out the door leaving me alone in the new house we had just built. Once again, I grieved--crying, screaming, not eating, and seeing him at my home group meeting with the new girlfriend, knowing he was right to end it but feeling wronged. Once again, consequences reared their ugly head, and he married the new girl.

It took me years to heal enough to go out on a date after that one, and that date was with none other than Mike Tracy, who always seemed to show up when I was down. He magically came around when Frank and I broke up, and now here he was again. Perhaps, one of the boys would mention it to him, I don't know, but here he was, again, and here I was again, crying about being dumped by another one. I would cry and he would call the guy an idiot and yell at me for going out with idiots. He would hold me, tell me how wonderful I was and how much he always loved me. I would let him hold me, stop crying, and we would profess our love to one another, joke about being eighty and sitting together in rocking chairs, and then say good by again.

Two months after Alex left, I became friends with a female minister. We went to the same woman's spiritual meeting every week, and I began to call her and share my pain with her. I felt as if she was an angel sent to me by God. When Alex left, he left everything, so there were loose ends. I had to gather all his things and put them in the basement, so I could not see them every day; however, when I stepped down into the basement and saw anything of his, the pain rushed in like a river. I needed him to take his things, but when I saw him or spoke to him, I froze and words disappeared. This minister began writing out the words for me to say to him, so I did not have to think. This worked, and eventually I gave him until the following Friday to pick up his things, or they would be out in the snow for anyone to take. By that Friday, he still had not come. Reluctantly, I put his stuff outside and called him. He came that evening. I stayed inside the house, not able to watch. This soft-spoken, loving minister was amazing, and I will always be grateful to her. God works in mysterious ways. Her name was Susan, and she was the woman Frank met the day I broke up with him. She was his wife.

CHAPTER 57

NEVER IS JUST AROUND THE CORNER

In 1997, I went to work for Shenandoah University. A few years before, the man that ran the International Programs at the university came to observe my class. I talked to him several times after that. The university wanted to start a new English as a Second Language program, so Bill asked me to help him design, and teach the classes. I was enrolled in a masters program there, but it was slow going because of the expense. Usually new employees at the school had to wait a year to receive free tuition. They agreed to waive the year, so I gladly accepted the position. The administrators and the principal, Larry, who hired me for Frederick County, were gracious. They agreed that it was a wonderful opportunity and let me out of my contract. One administrator said to me, "Take the job, and if you ever have a chance, come back to Frederick County and teach." I was overwhelmed by their kindness.

When I got sober, I did not trust people in authority, I did not believe people had my best interest at heart, and I did not think people did things in order to help another person. What a lesson I was learning; of course, I could not trust people when I was drinking. They were just like me—lying, selfish, self-centered law breaking people. Sobriety and risk taking rocketed me into a new dimension. Here were people who grew up, went to college, and knew how to give to others. All of this was foreign to me. I grew up damaged and learned to survive by running, lying, and escaping. On that first day of my sobriety, on, June 10, 1981, I entered Kindergarten and grew from there.

While not being in love, I achieved many things--a master's degree, four houses, and a real estate license. I completed credits for a doctorate in the Leadership in Education program and passed the final exam. All that was left to finish was the final paper.

On September 11, 2001, I was sitting in my office getting ready for my 9:30 AM class. I turned on the radio to catch the news and heard something about a plane crash. I turned the sound up and listened. The newscaster announced that a plane had just smashed into one of the twin tower buildings in New York City. I ran into my classroom, turned on the television and as my students streamed in, we sat in stunned silence trying to make sense of what we were seeing. One boy, cried, "Oh my God, my uncle was in that building. I have to call home."

"Go, I said, go call." He ran out of the room. We learned that there were two crashes and both towers were hit. I had no class that morning. We watched the events unfold on television and then talked about what we were feeling. Some students cried. I cried. Some asked to be excused and some were rooted to the television. Not one student wore the typical teenage bored or uninterested face. This event touched everyone everywhere and began a series of changes in many people's lives, including mine.

Immediately after this tragedy, most students from the Middle East were blocked from coming into the country; all visa rules were tightened, and the university lost many international students. Since most of my students were internationals my program along with many other English language programs in the country began to shrink. Within two years, my student population had shrunk to half of what it was prior to 2001.

One day, the dean called me into his office and told me that they were no longer able to justify the program as it stood. Due to the dwindling student numbers, my job would go from full time to part time. I felt lost, hurt, and angry even though there was nothing I could do about it. I knew I could not afford to work part time, so I made a decision to leave and go into real estate full time. I was 59 years old and three quarters of the way through my paper for my doctorate. During the course of my doctorate, I had been assigned three different advisors—one retired and two came and left within a short time. Every time a new advisor took over, their ideas of what this paper should be differed from the previous one. Hence, I had redone this paper several times. In addition, I had done a thesis paper for my masters but could not use it for the doctorate.

One morning in April, as I sat typing at 4:00 AM exhausted from work, stress, and pure age, a thought came to me, why am I doing this? I don't need this degree for anything I am going to do until I retire. I have proven I am not stupid. My grades throughout my nearly twenty years of school were always at the top of the class. I have already taken all the classes and passed the final exam. I know now that I am a successful person with enough intelligence to pass anything they throw at me academically, so this is enough. I knew that principal so long ago who told me I was not smart enough was wrong, and I knew within myself that I was not stupid, nor damaged, nor slow. My father was right, I was college material, and when I had the chance, I flew to the sky with it. Now, it was time to rest.

That morning I made an appointment with the latest advisor, went into his office, and told him I was not finishing the paper. He kindly tried to talk me out of it, telling me I was too close to being finished until I told him how old I was, how tired I was, and how I wanted to spend my time left writing what I loved.. I walked out of his office and felt lighter than I had in years! I had been working full time and going to school full time for almost twenty years and I was running out of age, but I felt wonderful. He told me I had seven years to finish the paper. I went home, tucked it neatly away in a drawer, and never looked back.

I applied to teach with Frederick County schools, and the same man who had hired me back in 1987, rehired me. As soon as the children entered the room, I felt at home. I always felt safe and secure with children. I felt drawn to them as they did to me. I had a lot to teach these children besides English. I taught some of my girls to be ladies, some of my boys to be proud of their country, family, and accomplishments. I was not able to tell them exactly where I came from, but I was able to share my son, Ricky's, story with them, to teach them about consequences of their actions. When I told my students I was leaving, several of the ones I had written detentions on cried, "but, you can't leave us, Ms. Huntley."

On June 7, 2003, exactly eight years and one month after Dad died, my mother died. She traveled to Florida with Venita in the winter and came home to Long Lake in the summer. Throughout the past ten years, she had become progressively sicker. Venita and her husband, Donny, were her caretakers. Today, I believe things happen for a reason, and it seems that Donny came along just at the right time to help care for my mother. He was wonderful to her, and I am so grateful to him for that. My sister took care of a father she despised because she knew how to do the right thing. She took care of my mother because she loved her and wanted the best for her in her last years. My sister naturally does the things I have had to painstaking learn to do. She is an amazing woman who I learn from everyday.

In spring of 2008, I received the inevitable "I am separated now" telephone call from Mike Tracy. I laughed. "What's so funny?" he said.

"For God's sake, Mike, how many times have you been separated now?"

He laughed, too, "I know, I know, but this time I really am."

"And," I said sarcastically.

"And, I want to get together and talk."

"About what?"

"I don't know; I guess about whatever. I need to talk. My job is driving me crazy. I think I'm going to quit."

"Good for you," I said knowing that his job was extremely stressful for him. He was a supervisor of a huge job. Mike made an enormous amount of money and had every toy imaginable, but he was not well. One year he called me saying that he was stuck in a motel room in Maryland and could not walk due to Gout. It was in the summer, so I went down and took care of him for two days until he was on his feet.

Once again, we met at his house in West Virginia. This time, he was officially divorced. We talked about getting back together. We saw each other awhile, but he still lived the old life and still drank, and I could not tolerate it. One day, I left him a note on his kitchen table telling him I could not be with him. He understood. We remain old friends, but another will fill the rocking chair beside him on his front porch.

CHAPTER 58

THE HOLIEST OF ALL SPOTS ON EARTH IS WHERE AN ANCIENT HATRED HAS BECOME A PRESENT LOVE.

I learned that I am not stupid. I learned that honor, pride, and courage come from doing right things. Today, when I share with a newcomer, "I did that, too," and I see relief in her eyes, I know that my life is a gift from God, and I am to use it to help others. I just celebrated thirty years of sobriety and as I accepted my chip, and looked out over the audience, I saw my son with 25 years and my brother with 20 years of sobriety. I am a loving grandmother today to Hannah, Daniel, and John. I teach my grandchildren about shooting a bow and arrow, climbing trees, and navigating wood trails. Today, their fathers are doing well—Ricky works in the computer field and is an outstanding musician. Monti is in the medical field, loves fishing, and hunting. One day I was a tornado leaving a path of destruction in people's lives. Today, I am a force for good.

My life was not the expected. It was not designed for me to skip along a golden path. I had to climb craggy cliffs and broken briars, but here I am at the top, gazing out my cabin window at Sabattis Mountain, the place I hid from the horrors of an alcoholic home.

My journey has humbled me. I stood on a lone precipice, magnificent in this new dimension of sobriety, and I jumped. I flew off that mountain, into life never looking back. Each day is the beginning of a new wonder. I jump out of bed, open the door, race down the steps and fly out the bee-lined path knowing I could be stung, living life to the fullest. I know I will do more; I will love more; I will give more. I am the daughter in full regalia, the sister who bonds in love, and the mother who stands steadfast. Most of my life, I fought the winds of God. The forces knocked me down. I got up again, willing myself to go on, struggling one step at a time, fighting all the way. Today, I ride the winds, zooming, dipping, and gliding, touching treasures along the way. Today I see you, today I see me, today I see.

Sedona and Grand Canyon trip, 1986

Tracy (niece), Linda, Aunt Sherry. House in San Diego.

Author and brother, Mike 2003

Ricky

Monti

Hannah

MY BEAUTIFUL GRANDCHILDREN

Daniel   John

REFERENCES

1. Burnett, C. (1932). Conquering the Wilderness. Norwood, MA: Pimpton Press.

2. Seaman, F (2002. Nehasane. Utica, NY: Nicholas K. Burns Publishing.

3. Timm, Ruth. (2007). Life in the Adirondacks. Utica, NY: Pyramid Publishing.

4. Williamson, Marianne. (1992). A Return to Love. .New York: Harper Collins.